# old testament roots of our faith

# old testament
# roots of our faith

## BY SISTER ELSPETH, O.A.S.

*Materials for Christian Education*
*Prepared at the Direction of General Convention*

## THE SEABURY PRESS
**GREENWICH • CONNECTICUT**

THE SEABURY SERIES is prepared for Christian education in parishes and missions by the National Council of the Protestant Episcopal Church in the United States of America at the direction of the General Convention.

THE REV. DAVID R. HUNTER, ED.D.
Director
Department of Christian Education

THE REV. WILLIAM SYDNOR, M.A.
Executive Secretary
Division of Curriculum Development

Chapter opening illustrations by Johannes Troyer
Maps by Leonard Derwinski

Library of Congress Catalogue Card Number: 57-8345

Scripture quotations are from the *Revised Standard Version of the Bible*, copyrighted 1946 and 1952 by the Division of Christian Education, National Council of Churches.

PRINTED IN THE UNITED STATES OF AMERICA

# contents

To the Reader                                        3


## Part One

### STORIES OF THE BEGINNING

1  The Story of Creation                             9
2  Cain and Abel                                    13
3  Noah and the Flood                               15
4  Sacred and Secular History                       20


## Part Two

### FAITH AND EXPERIENCE

5  Abraham                                          25
6  The Promises of God                              31
7  Isaac and Jacob                                  37
8  Joseph                                           44
9  The Escape from Egypt                            49
10 Building the Nation                              56
11 Entering the Promised Land                       64

v

12  Samson                          74
13  Samuel                          81
14  King Saul                       86
15  King David                      94
16  King Solomon                   104

## Part Three

### FAITH AND OBLIGATION

17  Elijah                         111
18  Elisha                         120
19  Amos                           126
20  Hosea                          131
21  Isaiah                         135
22  The Exile                      144
23  The New Israel                 150
24  Growing in Faith               157
25  The Letter to the Hebrews      163

    Index                          173

# list of maps

Abraham's World                             27

The Escape from Egypt                       54

Wandering in the Wilderness                 58

Entering the Promised Land                  66

Land of the Philistines—Palestine           76

David's Kingdom                             97

The Exile                                  147

vii

old testament roots of our faith

## TO THE READER

HAVE you ever wondered about the kind of people God chooses to do His work in the world? What do they have that you haven't? Do they ever do wrong? Do they make mistakes? Are they ever resentful and disagreeable? Do they find it hard to obey cheerfully?

There are some real answers to those questions in the stories in this book. Many of the chapters are short stories about individuals who had a hard time doing what God expected of them. But all the stories taken as a whole tell a much greater story than any single one. Instead of a lifetime, this bigger story covers all time. Instead of a hero, it tells of a people. Instead of a struggle between two men, it shows a struggle between mankind and God.

In the beginning, God gave man freedom to choose whether he would obey or do as he pleased, and the struggle has gone on ever since. God has never gone back on His gift of freedom, but He has acted all through time to win man to choose *His* way. God's purpose has remained steady as generation after generation has tried to live without Him, tried to compromise with His demands or find an easier way.

If you have not done much reading in the Bible, you might begin by looking up the references at the ends of paragraphs to see how the incident you have just read was told in the Bible itself. You may also want to investigate the suggestions for further reading, finding new Bible stories for yourself.

Few people have ever come to understand God's message just by reading the Bible. We all need people to talk things over with, to help us understand, and to add to what we already know. This is what you should be doing in your church school class, putting together your separate bits of information to make bigger bits, and finding out those ideas which need to be clarified.

Sister Elspeth, of the Anglican Order of All Saints, is the kind of person to whom people go with questions and doubts. She has given a long lifetime to reading and study, and she talks about Bible people as though they were old friends of hers, sometimes exasperating friends, but still lovable and real. This book has become a book because a tape recorder took down her stories and explanations as a church school teacher asked her questions. The teacher's questions were often ones that ninth-grade students had asked—and that you may be asking, too.

As you look at the chapter titles, you may wonder that so many of the stories come from the Old Testament; but as you read, you will begin to understand how the Old

Testament looks forward to the New Testament. Our relation to God is the theme of the whole Bible. The Act of the Incarnation was not a sudden event; it was the supreme outreach of the same loving God who, from the beginning, has been trying to help those who will not listen to Him, as well as those who long to hear.

PART ONE

STORIES OF THE BEGINNING

## CHAPTER I

## THE STORY OF CREATION

THE Bible is the best loved, most argued-about book in the world. During the past hundred years the Bible has been put through especially intensive and critical study. Scientific excavation of the lands of the Near East has added new knowledge which has had to be fitted into the total picture of ancient times. As a result, some ideas about the Bible have changed. The Bible, itself, is changeless. The more men study it, the more certain they become that (apart from the actual Incarnation of Jesus Christ) the Bible is the supreme revelation of God's love to man.

Most of our great-grandparents believed that everything in the Bible was written by direct dictation of the Holy Spirit; that every single word was literally true. Today some persons lean far in the other direction, calling the whole Bible "mere legend." What is the attitude of our

Church? Let's look at some of the books published by our National Council in recent years. *The Holy Scriptures,* by Robert C. Dentan, for example, justifies us in saying that few educated persons, if any, look on the first eleven chapters of Genesis as actual history. If they are read literally, these chapters say that the world was made in exactly six days, ending with the creation of the first man and woman, Adam and Eve.

The way we look at it is more like this. The first chapter of Genesis is the work of Hebrew writers who were trying to make their own people understand that God is the Creator and Ruler of the world, and that all their love and service should be given to Him. Those writers knew God in prayer with a truly personal knowledge, and they wanted others to know Him too.

The men who wrote the first book of the Bible were living in the midst of heathen nations who had already written childish and unworthy stories about the beginning of the world. The Biblical writers could not be sure, any more than we can, exactly when and how God created our universe; but writing with His help, they worked out a hymn of creation. The truth they made clear was that God created the world by the power of His Word, with no man's help. He worked in steps and stages, each step leading to the next. Sky was separated from earth, earth was separated from water. The earth was provided with vegetation and animals. Last of all, man, in God's own image and likeness, was created to serve and love Him.

There is nothing fanciful about the Biblical version of creation—as there often is in heathen myths about the world's beginning. Genesis makes it clear that God was making a home for man before placing man in it. The writers wanted us to see that the Creation was wholly in our behalf and that God had absolutely nothing to gain from it, a thought about the Divine purpose that is repeated in many of the psalms.

Man's part ever after was to serve God and develop the resources of the world. He was also given a free will to serve God, or to serve himself. This had to be, because man's service would have been worth nothing if he had been a mere machine wound up to act in a certain way, whether or not he wanted to. The Bible tells us that Adam, the first man, and Eve, the first woman, were tempted by a serpent and ate of the fruit of a forbidden tree. In Hebrew *Adam* means "Man" in general; *Eve* means "Life." God gave "Man" a choice. It is as if He said, "My way or your own." The story of Adam and Eve is the story of how man chose his own way and thought he knew better than God what was good for him.

So God took away the easy, pleasant life man had been living and led him into harder conditions where he might find out that he didn't know everything, and where he would learn that he needed God. The story of Adam and Eve is not history. It is what we call a parable. It is meant to show us how easy it is to sin, and how sin leads to separation from God. Although God sent Adam and Eve out of the garden, He was not being revengeful. His purpose was not to punish, but to teach. The whole Old Testament shows us God trying to win man back, of his own will, to an understanding relationship.

Around the Genesis story many myths and legends have sprung up. Some say the animals in the garden were at peace until Adam and Eve were banished; then the beasts began to quarrel and look on man as an enemy. According to another legend, Adam was allowed to bring out of Eden the branch of a tree. The story is that this branch was handed down from one generation to another, and that the patriarchs used it for blessing. The rod Moses carried to invoke the power of God was supposed to be this same branch. These stories are not in the Bible. They are interesting as folklore, but beyond that we don't need to be at all concerned with them. The lessons God wants us to learn are in the Bible. (Genesis 1–3)

## CHAPTER 2:

### CAIN AND ABEL

THE Cain and Abel story comes from the same background as the Creation stories. It is a story the Hebrew people had known for generations—a story they told over and over again around their campfires.

In the Garden of Eden story, Adam and Eve are represented as being alone. Later, when they lived outside the garden, there must have been other people. Cain and Abel, called by the Bible sons of Adam and Eve, represent the beginnings of social life. Cain was a farmer; Abel was a keeper of sheep. As such, the two men stand for two types of life not naturally in sympathy. They represent different cultures, different points of view. God wanted Cain and Abel to learn to understand and appreciate one another. From their story He wants *us* to learn that we have far-reaching social obligations.

The Bible tells us that: "In the course of time Cain brought to the LORD an offering of the fruit of the ground, and Abel brought of the firstlings of his flock and of their fat portions. And the LORD had regard for Abel and his offering, but for Cain and his offering he had no regard." The Bible does not tell us why God preferred Abel's sacrifice. Nor does it tell us precisely how God indicated his preference for Abel's offering. It does tell us that Cain was jealous, and that is the point of the story.

Cain's jealousy was not a momentary flicker of envy, but something on which Cain brooded until his love for his brother was turned to hate. Then he lured Abel to a deserted place and killed him.

But there is no spot so desolate that it is not under God's eye. And the LORD said, "Where is Abel your brother?"

"I do not know," Cain said. "Am I my brother's keeper?"

God's anger answered Cain's question. Cain *was* his brother's keeper. He was supposed to care what happened to Abel and to take responsibility for his brother's welfare. (Genesis 4:2–16)

Through this story God tells us that we are all our brothers' keepers. The word *brother* does not mean only a member of our family or church or neighborhood. When Jesus was asked the question, "Who is my neighbor," He answered by telling the story of the Good Samaritan. In this account the Samaritan stopped to bind the wounds of a man he had never seen before, a member of a hostile people. Everyone who needs our help is a brother, or neighbor, whose loving keeper God wants us to be. (St. Luke 10:29–37)

SUGGESTION FOR FURTHER READING: Genesis 11:1–10, the Hebrew explanation of why there are different peoples and languages on the earth.

CHAPTER 3:

NOAH AND THE FLOOD

FOR thousands of years, the little strip of coast we call
Palestine was surrounded by highly civilized empires—
Egypt, Assyria, Persia, Babylonia. Babylonia lay between
two great rivers—the Euphrates and the Tigris. You can
still find these rivers on the map. They empty into the
Persian Gulf. The land between them is now an independent Arab kingdom called Iraq. The Greeks called
this area Mesopotamia, "the land between the rivers."
Around 3000 B.C. the land between the Tigris and Euphrates was a good place to live in. It was crisscrossed
with irrigation ditches so that the wheat crop flourished
and boats were kept busy carrying grain and other prod-
ucts up and down the rivers. Great cities arose. One of
the earliest was called Ur.

In the Bible the city of Ur is called "Ur of the Chaldees"
because at one time the people who lived there were called

15

Chaldeans. You can go to Ur now quite comfortably by train. At the railroad station you will see "Ur Junction" posted on the wall. Walk out of the station, however, and you will see only a wide sandy waste. Twelve miles off grow green trees. In this country, greenery means water. Ur was green once. Then, about two thousand years ago, the river changed its course and a city was replaced by sand dunes with a single ruined tower sticking up in their midst.

In 1854 an Englishman living in Iraq got curious. He brought a few Arabs to the tower at Ur and directed them to dig into the tower's heart. Far below the surface they found clay tablets covered with writing. They dug deeper and uncovered lines of streets, temples, two-storied houses, schools. At this point, further excavation had to be postponed until after the First World War. When digging was resumed, more streets were uncovered. Then a layer of solid earth was reached. The archaeologists thought they had come to the bottom of everything, but, just to be sure, they went down eight feet lower and made an amazing discovery. There was another city below the first!

Here were wonderful tombs of kings and queens. The most notable was the tomb of Queen Shubad, who had been buried wearing a beautiful crown of beaten gold, set with jewels. Around her were the remains of court ladies and charioteers. The queen's harpist had a harp inlaid with mother-of-pearl and lapis lazuli, a beautiful semiprecious stone which is as blue as the sky and flecked with red and white and gold.

Two cities separated by a layer of mud! What could it mean? It meant that there must have been a great flood which had buried the lower city. No wonder so many tribes in neighboring lands had flood stories which they told and retold generation after generation. Many of these flood stories have been found in written form. One of the written versions, now in the British Museum in London, tells of a hero whose city the gods wished to destroy. One of the hero's gods told him to build a ship for himself and his family. The hero was also told to collect specimens of all living creatures. He obeyed, the story goes on, and the flood came. Finally a dove was sent out from the ship to see what was happening. The dove came back. A swallow was sent out next, but she also came back. Finally the man sent a raven; and when she did not return, the family came out of the ship and offered sacrifices, and "the gods smelled the sweet savor and gathered like flies over the sacrifices."

How like the Bible story of Noah! (Genesis 6–9) The two accounts are similar even at the end where, according to the heathen myth, "the goddess Ishtar lighted up a great rainbow."

Which story came first? It doesn't really matter. The important thing about the Bible story is the *meaning* the Hebrews gave to it. Unlike the other tribes of their day, the Hebrews did not worship a lot of quarreling gods and goddesses. Instead, they worshiped one God, who then—as now—required His people to serve Him not only with sacrifices and gifts but also with righteous lives.

When the Israelites were taken to Babylon as captives from 597 to 586 (remember that time before Christ, B.C., seems to move in reverse order—the higher number is the older date; the lower number is nearer our day), they must have heard the Babylonian flood story. They may have compared it with their own tale of Noah. We can imagine them saying, "We know that the flood didn't depend on the whim of heathen gods. It came for the same reason that we Hebrews are here in Babylon—because of sin. When we have done our penance, God will show mercy on us again. We shall be his people still when these heathens are all buried in the ruins of Babylon!"

Below the flood level Queen Shubad lies. With her are the ladies who were put to death merely to provide a queen with an escort into the next world. A city of luxury and tyranny is covered with mud. But a rainbow, the symbol of God's promise to be merciful, arches over the children of God forever.

"Behold," the LORD says in the ninth chapter of Genesis, "I establish my covenant with you and your descendants after you. . . . I set my bow in the cloud, and it shall be a sign of the covenant between me and the earth."

The story of Noah shows men increasing in wickedness, falling away from God, closing their ears to God's word. But, as always all through the Bible, there are men like Noah who refuse to be drawn into sin. They represent God's faithful servants in every generation. Noah lived to lay the foundations of a better world. The story makes no attempt to answer the question often asked today:   Why must the innocent suffer along with the wicked? The Bible finds it enough to say that those who do serve God are taken care of in God's way.

THE *National Geographic Magazine* for January, 1930, has an article on the excavations at Ur. It is called "New

Light on Ancient Ur" and is written by M. E. L. Mal-
lowan. If your library keeps bound copies of back issues
of the *Geographic*, look up this article, for it includes
pictures of some of the things mentioned in this chapter
and a quotation from the Babylonian story of the flood.

## CHAPTER 4:

### SACRED AND SECULAR HISTORY

ONE of the things we learn from the Bible is that there is a difference between sacred and secular history. Sacred history is the story of man's redemption: that is, of the process by which God plans to bring all mankind back to Himself. The Old Testament is the story of some of the people God chose to carry out His plan. God works through people; all through history it has been His method to save the many through the few. And the few sometimes take a lot of urging—as we can see today.

Secular history seldom says anything about the purposes of God. It just reports the succession of events from the beginning of time up to the present. The stories reported in our daily newspapers are the latest chapters of secular history, and history books record the early chapters. Some of these past events are mentioned in the Bible also. At the times when Egypt, Babylonia, and the other great empires of the Eastern Mediterranean came into contact with the chosen people of God, sacred and secular history overlapped.

In the Bible, sacred history runs like a scarlet thread through the fabric of secular history, touching it here and there, drawing it within the purpose of God. In Isaiah, for example, God reveals to the prophet that He is using the Assyrians "to be the rod of my anger" to bring the people to repentance. Again in Isaiah God says that He has "called" Cyrus, King of Persia, to send the Hebrews back to their own land. Yet while Egypt, Assyria, and Babylonia furthered God's purpose almost without knowing that they were doing so, they never accepted Jehovah as their God; and, alas, the Hebrews never fulfilled their missionary vocation to bring others to the worship of the one true God. (Isaiah 10 and 45)

Yet in spite of human failures, the will of God *was* done. For two thousand years God gave His people a succession of leaders and prophets who called them back and back again to the fulfillment of their destiny. With infinite patience God led His children at last to Bethlehem. The first Christmas was a long time coming.

The great story of the preparation for the Gospel is called the Old Testament. The story of the redeeming acts of Jesus Christ and of the establishment of the Church to carry out the purposes of God is found in the New Testament. This, too, is part of sacred history.

PART TWO

# faith and experience

# CHAPTER 5:

## ABRAHAM

THE faith of the Hebrew people begins with the call of Abraham, the legendary father of the people.

We are told in the book of Genesis that Abraham (or Abram, as he was then called) lived first in the city of Ur by the river Euphrates. Abraham's family was probably one of a group of Hebrew families who had been settled there for some time, keeping their flocks and herds outside the city. It is implied that they were not of the same race or religion as the men of Ur who worshiped many gods. What was said in Chapter 3 of this book about the excavations on the site of the city of Ur is a matter of secular history. The call that came to Abraham in Ur is sacred history.

One day there came to Abraham a call from the one true God. "Go from your country and your kindred and your father's house to the land that I will show you," God

25

said. "And I will make of you a great nation, and I will bless you, and make your name great, so that you will be a blessing." Whether the words came to Abraham as a dream or a vision we do not know. We do know that Abraham did as he was told. (Genesis 12:1,2)

First he had to travel northward up the river to a place called Haran, where Abraham's father died. Then he turned south into the land of Canaan, now called Palestine. There, in a great and solemn scene, God promised Abraham the whole land for his descendants, and Abraham dedicated himself to the lifelong service of God.

For there was a condition attached to God's promise: "Walk before me, and be blameless." (Genesis 17:1) That was a new thing in the world in the second millennium before Christ. The gods of the nations round about were worshiped with costly sacrifices, but none of them asked their followers to lead an especially good life. From the very first, the Hebrews were required to love God.

Traveling with Abraham was a young man named Lot, the son of Abraham's brother. (Genesis 12:5) Both Lot and Abraham had so many flocks and herds and tents, "that the land could not support both of them dwelling together . . . and there was strife between the herdsmen of Abram's cattle and the herdsmen of Lot's cattle. . . . Then Abram said to Lot, 'Let there be no strife between you and me. . . . Is not the whole land before you? Separate yourself from me. If you take the left hand, then I will go to the right; or if you take the right hand, then I will go to the left.' And Lot lifted up his eyes, and saw that the Jordan valley was well watered everywhere like the garden of the LORD. . . . So Lot chose for himself all

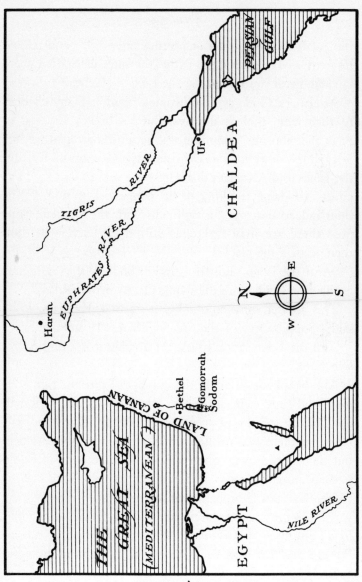

ABRAHAM'S WORLD

the Jordan valley, and Lot journeyed east . . . and moved his tent as far as Sodom. Now the men of Sodom were wicked, great sinners against the LORD." (Genesis 13:5–13)

As always, God gave the people of Sodom many chances to turn from their evil ways. But sin breeds sin, and in time neighboring communities became outraged at the wickedness of Sodom and its sister city, Gomorrah. Finally, the LORD told Abraham that He was going to destroy both cities. Abraham, thinking of his nephew, Lot, said, "Wilt thou indeed destroy the righteous with the wicked? Suppose there are fifty righteous within the city; wilt thou then destroy the place?"

"And the LORD said, 'If I find at Sodom fifty righteous in the city, I will spare the whole place for their sake.' "

This answer came so quickly it startled Abraham, so he said, "Suppose five of the fifty righteous are lacking?"

And the LORD said, "I will not destroy it if I find forty-five there."

Abraham kept reducing the number of possible righteous men, and God kept agreeing. "For the sake of ten I will not destroy it," the LORD promised. Finally Abraham realized that there was no limit to God's mercy and patience, but that there was no one really good there but Lot, so he said no more. (Genesis 18:20–33)

Step by step, Abraham was learning more about God's ways. He grew to be sure that God would never ask him to do anything that would not bring a blessing in return. But the real test was yet to come. Abraham and his wife, Sarah, had one son, Isaac, born late in their lives, whom they both loved deeply. One day God said to Abraham,

"Take your son . . . and go to the land of Moriah, and offer him there as a burnt offering upon one of the mountains of which I shall tell you." Abraham had learned to trust God, and God had never failed him. But this time Abraham must have had a terrible struggle with the temptation to rebel. Yet, as Jesus did years later, Abraham decided, "Not my will, but thine."

So we see an old man and a boy walking quietly to the place appointed for the sacrifice. Before they get there, Abraham tells the servants not to follow him any farther. He is afraid they may protest, and make it harder for him and for his son. The words of the Bible are better than anything we could make up. "And Abraham took the wood of the burnt offering, and laid it on Isaac his son; and he took in his hand the fire and the knife. So they went both of them together." Abraham was so quiet and calm that the child had no suspicion his father's heart was close to breaking.

"And Isaac said to his father Abraham, 'My father!'"

"And he said, 'Here am I, my son.'"

"He said, 'Behold, the fire and the wood; but where is the lamb for a burnt offering?'"

"Abraham said, 'God will provide himself the lamb for a burnt offering, my son.'"

". . . When they came to the place of which God had told him, Abraham built an altar there, and laid the wood in order, and bound Isaac his son, and laid him on the altar, upon the wood. Then Abraham put forth his hand, and took the knife to slay his son. But the angel of the LORD called to him from heaven . . . 'Do not lay your hand on the lad or do anything to him; for now I know that you fear God, seeing you have not withheld your son, your only son, from me.'" (Genesis 22:1–12)

It is not strange, is it, that in days long after, when his descendants wrote down his story, they called Abraham the "Friend of God"?

In the dark years that followed, when Abraham's descendants found it difficult to obey God, they always felt that their forefather was the model Hebrew, the man of perfect faith. After all, here was a man who believed God's word even when it seemed to fail; a man who obeyed even when God seemed to contradict Himself.

Abraham is also often called "father" by the great leaders and prophets. Zechariah, father of St. John the Baptist, recalls in the Christian hymn called the Benedictus, "the oath which he sware to our forefather Abraham." And the Virgin Mary, in the hymn we call the Magnificat, says, "As he promised to our forefathers, Abraham and his seed for ever." (St. Luke 1:55, 73)

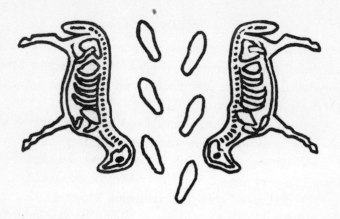

## CHAPTER 6:

### THE PROMISES OF GOD

God had a special job picked out for Abraham. He wanted Abraham to be the forefather of a holy people—God's special treasure among nations. When Abraham first came into the Promised Land (though not a single square inch of it belonged to him then), God wanted him to know that he had not come there for himself alone, but had come to be the founder of a great people. To emphasize this, the consecration of Abraham and his reception of God's promise were carried out by means of a solemn ceremony.

Abraham had to choose certain animals out of his flock and bring them to an appointed place and cut them in half. He laid them down on the ground and separated the halves in such a way that he could walk between them. This was a common method of sealing a bargain in those days. (If two men wanted to make an agreement, they would walk between the halves of a sacrificed animal. The meaning was that the agreement was as unchangeable as if they had been dead.) In this case, the ritual was a hundred times more solemn because it symbolized an agreement between Abraham and God.

Abraham separated his animals and laid them down. All day long he waited beside them. Again and again he had to beat off swooping birds of prey. As darkness fell, Abraham went into a kind of trance. In the midst of a horrible darkness, he felt a frightening sense of awe. He saw a light shining like a furnace. Then he saw a torch, with no hand to hold it, passing between the halves of the sacrificed animals. Abraham trembled, knowing he was in the presence of God. That was God's sign of the covenant. Then a voice said to him, "To your descendants I give this land."

"To your descendants I give this land." That was God's part of the covenant, and Abraham and his sons after him all felt that it was one of the most solemn promises that had ever been made. (Genesis 15:9–19)

Now the promise, of course, put certain conditions on the people. They had to be true to their part of the agreement, which was to love God and serve Him. After a time they began to neglect their obligations. But each time, the LORD God had mercy on them and sent them a great deliverer to help them make a fresh start in obedience. Moses, Joshua, David, and ever so many prophets were sent by God to point out to the people their duty and to remind them of their side of the promise.

Generations after the time of Abraham, when the Hebrews came to have kings, the kings were meant to be leaders, too. But even the kings often failed to keep the promise of obedience to God. At last things became so bad that the Hebrews had to be taught a great lesson. They had to learn to value the Promised Land—by losing it. They were all carried away to Babylon. (Chapter 22 of this book tells about their exile.)

But there were always some Hebrews who remained loyal to God. Even in Babylon, they were fixed in their minds that God would never break His part of the promise, that in some way or other He would renew it for them and make it true again. He would do as He had in the past and send them a great deliverer. That was really the beginning of the Hebrew people's belief in the Messianic promise.

*Messiah* originally meant "anointed" or "the anointed one." The Jews used to anoint their kings and their priests, and sometimes their prophets, with sacred oils which were carefully made. These oils were symbolic of God's gift of power for the office. An anointed person was regarded as sacred and chosen by God for a particular purpose. But from the time of their captivity on, the Hebrews had no powerful kings, and they didn't know how the deliverer would come.

They went into captivity in 586, and they were in Babylon a little less than fifty years. In 538, Cyrus, King of Persia, allowed them to go back to Israel—back to the Promised Land. When they got there, the Hebrews put their government into the hands of priests. It must have occurred to many believers at this point that if their deliverer were not to be a king, perhaps he would be a priest.

But while the priests should have been godly men, they

often were not. The people were forced to revise their ideas again. Now many of them hoped not for a king or a priest, but for someone straight from heaven, sent by God to be their deliverer.

At last the Jews were learning what God wanted them to learn, but even at the time our Lord lived on earth, people were mixed up as to who He was. You may remember that our Lord Himself asked the priests, "What do you think of Christ?" What He was saying was, "What do you think of the Messiah?" for the word *Christ* is the Greek form of "Messiah." (When we say "Jesus Christ," we mean "Jesus Messiah." So did the apostles when they began to preach.) (St. John 4:25–26)

At the time of the birth of Christ, Palestine had been part of the Roman Empire for over sixty years. Its priestly rulers had ceased to care about anything except keeping themselves in power by pleasing the Romans. There was little room in their hearts and minds for the idea of a Messiah. But the hope was still a reality to many who clung to the belief that their deliverer would be a "son of David."

Some of the most thoughtful Jews living at the time of Jesus were Galileans. The disciples came from Galilee, and there were many others from that area who followed Jesus. Nazareth was in Galilee, and when John the Baptist was born, and when the angel told Mary about the Child she was to bear, all these things were talked about by those who were looking for redemption in Israel. But it was not geography that united the group which was to be the nucleus of the Christian Church. It was belief in God's

promise of redemption and a Messiah. This fact is important, because there are people who think we Christians got
together because we *admired* our Lord. The real beginning
of Christianity was the shared certainty that God had sent
the Christ, the Messiah.

How strong the feeling of the promise was! Paul, on
trial before Festus, says, "My manner of life from my
youth, spent from the beginning among my own nation
and at Jerusalem, is known by all the Jews. They have
known for a long time, if they are willing to testify, that
according to the strictest party of our religion I have lived
as a Pharisee. And now I stand here on trial for hope in the
promise made by God to our fathers, to which our twelve
tribes hope to attain, as they earnestly worship night and
day. . . . To this day I have had the help that comes from
God, and so I stand here testifying both to small and great,
saying nothing but what the prophets and Moses said
would come to pass: that the Christ must suffer, and that,
by being the first to rise from the dead, he would proclaim
light both to the people and to the Gentiles." (Acts
26:4-7,22-23)

That was the message of the Christian Church all
through the New Testament—that they were not preaching
a new faith, but that Jesus who died and rose again was
the long-promised Messiah.

Present-day Jewish teaching denies that Jesus was the
Messiah. Some Jews still hope *for* a Messiah. There is a
pathetic story that during World War II, when the
Germans were shipping Jews to concentration camps by
the thousands, an allied prisoner saw a group of Jewish

girls being loaded into the trucks which were to cart them away. The girls were singing, "What shall we do when Messiah comes?"

In recent years, many Jews have turned their eyes toward another form of promised land: Israel, a spot on the map to call their own.

CHAPTER 7:

ISAAC AND JACOB

ABRAHAM's story is the key to all that follows. This is so because of his faith—the faith which he shared with Isaac and Jacob. Abraham was a man any people might honor and be glad to claim as their founder. We cannot say as much of his immediate descendants, however. Isaac, his son, is a rather colorless figure. Jacob, Isaac's son, was mean and dishonorable—at least at the beginning of his life. But God works with men as He finds them. According to His purpose, He trains His instruments to take their places in the grand scheme of the universe. This was His way with Jacob.

Isaac actually had two sons—twins named Jacob and Esau. Esau, a great, hairy, rough fellow, who was fond of hunting, was always out in the fields. Jacob was more inclined to stay home and look after things for his mother. Isaac was proud of his big, outdoor boy, Esau, and he made no secret of enjoying the deer meat Esau brought home from his hunting trips. One day, Esau returned from a hunt ravenously hungry. He found Jacob sitting on a stool near the house cutting beans to make soup. "Oh, give me some," cried Esau. "I'm about to die of hunger."

Jacob, who had always resented being younger and less the apple of his father's eye than was Esau, said craftily, "I will give you some of my soup if you will give me your birthright."

"What do I care about my birthright, when I am nearly dead of hunger?" Esau said, in his offhand way. Of course, he wasn't anywhere near being dead. He had just been outdoors all day and had worked up a good appetite. But because he was the sort of devil-may-care fellow he was, he said, "Here, you can have the birthright . . . give me the soup." He had his soup, but the Bible sums up the matter very severely, "Thus Esau despised his birthright." (Genesis 25:27–34)

From that time on, Jacob and his mother began to scheme how they could get Isaac's deathbed blessing for Jacob. The blessing meant something special. In those days when the Hebrews had neither kings nor priests, they had enormous respect for the father of a family. They believed that God gave a father special power and that the last blessing a father gave to his child would surely come true. By tradition this blessing went to the eldest son.

One day Isaac, who had grown old and was now nearly blind, said to Esau, "Go out in the fields and get some game and bring in a nice dish of hot meat, and then I will give you my blessing."

Rebecca, Isaac's wife, overheard; and as soon as Esau

had gone, she called her son Jacob and said, "Go to the flock and get me two plump, young kids, and I will cook them up just the way your father likes, and you can take the dish in to him." She knew that Isaac could not see well enough to tell his sons apart by sight.

"But," said Jacob, "I am a smooth man, and Esau is all hairy." He was thinking that his father might reach out and touch him.

But Rebecca had a solution for this, too. She took the skin of one of the kids Jacob killed, and she wrapped it around Jacob's hands and neck so that they would feel rough and hairy like Esau's. Then she put Esau's clothes on Jacob so that Jacob even smelled like Esau.

Still, Isaac was suspicious. Perhaps it was Jacob's voice which made the father ask dubiously, "Are you my very son Esau?"

Jacob said, "Yes, I am."

Then Isaac ate the meat, and when he had finished he gave Jacob the official family blessing which carried with it title to everything that belonged to the family then and in time to come.

A short while later, in came Esau with the dish of meat he had prepared. Isaac said, "Who are you?"

Esau said, "I am your son Esau."

Then Isaac realized that he had been deceived, and he said, "I have already given the blessing to your brother."

"Can't you give me a blessing too?" Esau asked.

But Isaac said that he had given his word and could not undo it. Now if you stop to think about it, a man like Esau, who would give away his birthright for a bowl of soup, probably was not the right man to carry the responsibilities of family leadership. Although Jacob's act of deceit was entirely wrong, it is still true that God recognized him as the heir of the family and of His promise to his forefather Abraham.

As we read history, we find that over and over again God chooses people to carry out parts of His will, and He uses them as they are because of certain gifts they have. But from the moment He chooses them, He begins to help them remold their lives. So it was with Jacob and with his son Joseph after him.

Jacob got little immediate pleasure from his inheritance. Rebecca suffered, too, as you can tell by her advice to Jacob. "Behold, your brother Esau comforts himself by planning to kill you," she said. "Now therefore, my son, obey my voice; arise, flee to Laban my brother in Haran, and stay with him a while, until your brother's fury turns away. . . . Why should I be bereft of you both in one day?" Then Rebecca told Isaac that Jacob should leave before he married a neighboring girl. Isaac was also anxious that his heir choose a desirable bride. (Genesis 27)

So Jacob headed north to Haran. On the way he was lonely and miserable, conscious of having done wrong, unable to undo what he had done. At nightfall he stopped at Bethel, where his grandfather Abraham had once built a shrine. (See the map on page 27.)

Exhausted, Jacob lay down on the bare ground, a stone for his pillow, and fell asleep. "And he dreamed that there was a ladder set up on the earth, and the top of it reached to heaven; and behold, the angels of God were ascending and descending on it!" Then the voice of God said, "Behold, I am with you and will keep you wherever you go. . . ." (Genesis 28:10–17)

Jacob, who up to now had given little thought to God, was filled with awe. "Surely," he said, "the LORD is in this place." God had forgiven Jacob, but He had not finished teaching and reshaping him. Jacob was to find out what it felt like to be deceived and to have to work for what he wanted.

When he finally reached Haran, where his uncle lived, he found that Laban had two daughters, Leah and Rachel. Rachel was very beautiful, and Jacob fell in love with her and asked Laban if he might marry her. Laban saw a chance to make a profit. He got Jacob to agree to work for him for seven years to win Rachel.

Jacob served the seven years and the Bible says "they seemed to him but a few days because of the love he had for her." At the end of the seven years, a great feast was held and the marriage ceremony was performed. According to Eastern custom, the bride was heavily veiled. After the ceremony, she was brought to Jacob's tent, but he was not allowed to remove her veil until the following day. When Jacob did unveil his bride, behold, it was Leah!

Jacob rushed to Laban and said, "What is this you have done to me? Did I not serve with you for Rachel? Why then have you deceived me?"

Laban answered, "It is not so done in our country, to give the younger before the first-born."

Outraged as he was, Jacob must have realized that he was getting the same treatment he had given his father. He said to Laban, "Couldn't I have Rachel, too?" (In those days it was not unlawful to have several wives.)

Laban said, "Yes, you can have Rachel, but you will have to serve me another seven years." (Genesis 29:1–28)

So Jacob served Laban another seven years. Even then

Jacob did not leave for home, because he and Laban could not agree on the question of wages which were to be paid in flocks and herds. After another six years, this argument, too, was settled; and Jacob started home.

Along the way Jacob met messengers who told him that Esau was approaching with four hundred men. "Then Jacob was greatly afraid and distressed; and he divided the people that were with him, and the flocks and herds and camels, into two companies, thinking, 'If Esau comes to the one company and destroys it, then the company which is left will escape.' " (Genesis 32:7–8)

"Deliver me," Jacob prayed, "from the hand of my brother . . . lest he come and slay us all, the mothers with the children." From the herds and flocks he had with him, Jacob took "two hundred she-goats and twenty he-goats, two hundred ewes and twenty rams, thirty milch camels and their colts, forty cows and ten bulls, twenty she-asses and ten he-asses." These he sent to Esau, hoping the handsome present might appease him. But there was no need for a gift. Esau ran to meet Jacob and "embraced him, and fell on his neck and kissed him, and they wept." (Genesis 32:11–16; 33:1–4)

As Jacob looked back on all that happened, he remembered how God had spoken to him when he fled from his brother years before. He returned to Bethel, the place of his vision, and built an altar there "to the God who answered me in the day of my distress and has been with me wherever I have gone."

When Jacob came to Bethel God again spoke to him. This time He repeated to him the promise made to his grandfather, Abraham: "The land which I gave to Abraham and Isaac I will give to you, and I will give the land to your descendants after you." From this time on Jacob was to be called by a new name, Israel, and his twelve sons were to be the founders of the "Twelve Tribes of Israel." All Hebrews after this were members of one of the twelve tribes, or families, and each traced its ancestry back to Abraham through one of the sons of Jacob. (Genesis 35)

## CHAPTER 8:

### JOSEPH

Jacob had twelve sons. Some of them were Leah's sons, but Joseph was the son of Rachel. Jacob loved Joseph so dearly that he was inclined to spoil him. He let him have his own way and gave him all sorts of presents. It is not surprising that after a while Joseph's brothers began to hate him, especially because Joseph himself grew conceited and disagreeable. He thought he was somebody special. He once told his family that he had dreamed the sun and moon and eleven stars had come down and bowed before him. Even Jacob took exception to that dream. He said, "What? Shall I and your mother and your brothers indeed come to bow ourselves to the ground before you?" Naturally Joseph's brothers were angrier than ever.

Shortly after this incident, the brothers went off into the country to see about the shearing of their flocks. After

44

a day or two Jacob asked Joseph to find his brothers and
see how they were getting on. Joseph set out, wearing a
coat his father had given him. The coat was expensive
and beautiful. Somehow this fine coat seemed to symbolize
to the brothers all the special favors Joseph had received.
So when they saw him coming, they felt this was their
chance to get rid of him. "Here comes this dreamer," they
cried. "Let us kill him." They decided to tell their father
that wild animals had eaten Joseph.

When Joseph came near, his brothers seized him and
pulled off his coat. But there was some argument as to how
to kill the boy. Two of the brothers didn't like the job at
all. Unable to decide what to do, they threw Joseph into
a deep pit and continued to argue. A caravan of merchants
bound for Egypt happened to pass by just then, and it
occurred to the brothers that they might sell Joseph. They
did—for twenty pieces of silver. So Joseph was taken away
to Egypt.

The brothers killed a goat and smeared the blood over
Joseph's coat and brought it to Jacob. He recognized it
immediately. "It is my son's robe," he cried. "A wild beast
has devoured him." For many days Jacob wept and refused
to be comforted. (Genesis 37)

In Egypt Joseph was sold for a slave to Potiphar, a
captain of the king's guard. By now Joseph had begun to
realize that he was not as important as he had imagined.
He served Potiphar loyally and intelligently and in time
was put in charge of the captain's entire estate. Handsome
and capable, Joseph was admired by many—including
Potiphar's wife, who decided she was in love with him.

He would have nothing to do with her. This so angered the lady that she went to Potiphar with false tales about Joseph. "The Hebrew servant, whom you have brought among us, came in to insult me," she said. Potiphar was furious and ordered Joseph to be cast into prison.

But even imprisonment was part of God's plan. In the prison, Joseph's qualities of leadership were again recognized, and he was put in charge of the other prisoners. He also acquired a reputation for interpreting dreams. (Genesis 39)

One night the king of Egypt had a puzzling dream. When none of his servants could say what the dream meant, Pharaoh sent for Joseph. "I have heard it said of you that when you hear a dream you can interpret it."

Joseph answered, "It is not in *me;* God will give Pharaoh a favorable answer."

Pharaoh told Joseph his dream: "Behold, in my dream I was standing on the banks of the Nile; and seven cows, fat and sleek, came up out of the Nile and fed in the reed grass; and seven other cows came up after them, poor and very gaunt and thin. . . . And the thin and gaunt cows ate up the first seven fat cows, but when they had eaten them no one would have known that they had eaten them, for they were still as gaunt as at the beginning. Then I awoke." Pharaoh then told another dream in which he had seen seven full strong ears of corn eaten up by seven thin, blighted ears of corn.

Joseph told Pharaoh that his two dreams were saying the same thing. They were a warning that after seven years of good harvest, Egypt would suffer seven years of famine. Knowing this beforehand, the sensible thing to do would be to store up food during the seven good years so that when the famine came there would be reserve supplies to draw upon.

Pharaoh was so pleased with Joseph that he said, "Since God has shown you all this . . . you shall be over my house," and he made Joseph a kind of prime minister.

His confidence was well placed. Joseph did such a good job of stockpiling produce that, when the lean years came, there was enough food not only for Egypt but also for foreigners who came to buy. Since the famine had blighted most of the countries bordering Egypt, Pharaoh's court-yard was almost always filled with men asking Joseph for food. (Genesis 41)

Eventually Joseph's own family ran out of food. Jacob said to his sons, "I have heard that there is grain in Egypt; go down and buy grain for us there."

The brothers went to the Egyptian palace, and were received by a regal-looking official dressed in fine linen, wearing a gold chain around his neck and the Pharaoh's own signet ring on his finger. Although they had not the slightest idea who he was, Joseph recognized his brothers almost immediately. Years before, he might have wanted to pay them back for what they had done to him. Now he was very kind to them, and arranged for the whole family —seventy people—to come to Egypt where Pharaoh gave them a strip of good land near the border.

But Jacob's family never forgot the covenant Abraham had made with God, the promise of the land. When Jacob died he asked his sons to carry him all the way back into the land of Canaan to bury him in the same cave where Abraham and Isaac and their wives were buried. Joseph continued to care for his brothers and their families as long as he lived.

And so, by strange and roundabout paths, a conceited boy came to hold a high position in which he could help many people. Best of all, Joseph changed *inside*, so that he was able to say to his brothers, "You meant evil against me; but God meant it for good." (Genesis 50)

SUGGESTION FOR FURTHER READING: Genesis 42–45, how Joseph tested his brothers when they came to Egypt.

## CHAPTER 9:

### THE ESCAPE FROM EGYPT

SOMETIME after the death of Joseph there was a change of dynasty in Egypt, and the new king was fearful of the foreigners living within the borders of his country. He enslaved the Hebrews and made them work for him.

But the more they were afflicted, the stronger and more numerous the Hebrew people seemed to be. There came a time when the Egyptians began to think that there were too many Hebrews in Egypt, even though they were slaves. "Behold," the Egyptian king said, "the people of Israel are too many and too mighty for us. Come, let us deal shrewdly with them, lest they multiply, and, if war befall us, they join our enemies and fight against us. . . ." Thereupon he gave orders that every Hebrew boy should be killed at birth. (Exodus 1)

At risk of her own life, one Hebrew mother hid her baby for three months. Unable to hide him any longer, she made a basket of rushes, daubed it with pitch to make it watertight, and placed the baby in it, among the reeds at the edge of the river. She stationed the baby's sister nearby to watch and see what would happen.

Pharaoh's daughter came to the river to bathe. Seeing the basket, she sent her maid to fetch it. The maid waded out and brought the basket back to the princess who looked in, saw the baby, and took pity on him. Eagerly, the baby's sister hurried over and said, "Shall I go and call you a nurse from the Hebrew women to nurse the child for you?"

The princess said yes, and the baby's own mother came to nurse him.

Moses, as Pharaoh's daughter named the baby, grew up in the royal household. He had every princely advantage. And through his real mother, he also knew the history of his own people and was saddened by their suffering.

One day Moses saw an Egyptian man beating a Hebrew slave. In fury he killed the Egyptian and hid the body in the sand. Very soon the crime was discovered, and Moses had to leave Egypt. He went to Midian, the site of Mount Horeb (also called Mount Sinai). (Exodus 2:1–21)

In Midian, Moses married and settled down to herding his father-in-law's sheep. He tried not to think about the Hebrews in Egypt because there seemed to be no way he could help them. But one day, as Moses watched his flocks near the foot of Mount Horeb, he suddenly saw a bush on fire. Running to look at it, he was astonished to see that although the flame leaped and crackled, while smoke rose, the branches of the bush remained whole and unburned. Moses sensed that this was a wonder, and that he was supposed to learn something from it. So he went up a little closer still, and a voice spoke to him out of the bush and said, "Do not come near; put off your shoes from your feet, for the place on which you are standing is holy ground." Then Moses knew it was the voice of God and fell down on his face on the ground. The fact that Moses recognized God's presence is emphasized in the Bible, which says, "When the LORD saw that he *turned aside to see*, God called to him out of the bush, 'Moses, Moses!'"

Moses answered, "Here am I."

The Lord said, "I am the God of your father, the God of Abraham, the God of Isaac, and the God of Jacob. . . . I have seen the affliction of my people who are in Egypt. . . . Come, I will send you to Pharaoh that you may bring forth my people, the sons of Israel, out of Egypt."

When Moses heard this, he was afraid. He had tried to help one Hebrew and had been forced to run for his life. The job of helping all the Hebrews seemed impossible. He began to make excuses. He said he could not speak well, that he was afraid the people would not believe him.

God overruled all objections. He said, "Say this to the people of Israel, 'The LORD, the God of your fathers, the God of Abraham, the God of Isaac, and the God of Jacob, has sent me to you.'" Moses knew that the Hebrews, living among people who worshiped many gods, each with a name, would need a name for *their* God, so he said, "If I come to the people of Israel and say to them, 'The God of your fathers has sent me to you,' and they ask me, 'What is his name?' what shall I say to them?" God told Moses the people were to call Him Jehovah, which means "I AM WHO I AM."[1]

---

[1] The word LORD when spelled with capital letters, stands for the divine name, YHWH, or Jehovah.

Still Moses hung back, so God told him his brother Aaron, who was a good speaker, could go with him and help him. (Exodus 3 and 4)

Then Moses returned to Egypt, and he and Aaron went to Pharaoh and said, "Thus says the LORD, the God of Israel, 'Let my people go.'"

Pharaoh asked, "Who is the LORD, that I should heed his voice and let Israel go? I do not know the LORD, and moreover I will not let Israel go." Moses warned Pharaoh that he could not ignore God's will without suffering bitter consequences. But Pharaoh scoffed and abused the Hebrews more than he had before.

Then things began to happen. Swarms of flies and gnats and frogs plagued the Egyptians. A hailstorm ruined the corn and wheat. In the wake of the hail came swarms of locusts which ate all the plants and fruit which the hail had not damaged. "Not a green thing remained through all the land of Egypt," the Bible says. The Nile River became polluted and poisonous. Disease killed the Egyptians' cattle, their horses, camels, sheep, and goats.

Each time disaster struck, Pharaoh would get frightened and say that he would let the Israelites go. But when the trouble grew less, he would go back on his promise. At last God told Moses that Pharaoh would not get any more chances to say no.

Now Moses was a sensible man, and he had no doubt been preparing his people for a long time, saying something like, "One of these days we will have to go, so you must always be ready to leave." It would be no easy matter to get twelve tribes of people under way, especially with the flocks and herds that they would need. But Moses had instructed the chief men, the heads of tribes, and assigned them to pass along the word to start. He had only to relay God's instructions to them.

When the time came, Moses told each family to sacrifice a lamb and eat it all. Then they were to stand with their staves in their hands, their sandals on their feet, and to have all their baggage ready to move at a moment's notice. Most important of all, they were to take some of the blood from the sacrificed lamb and spatter it on the doorposts of each house. "For the LORD will pass through to slay the Egyptians; and when he sees the blood on the . . . two doorposts, the LORD will pass over the door, and will not allow the destroyer to enter your houses to slay you."

At midnight, the LORD killed all the first-born children in the land of Egypt, "from the first-born of Pharaoh who sat on his throne to the first-born of the captive who was in the dungeon." But He passed over the homes of the Hebrews. In remembrance of this episode, the Hebrews have celebrated the feast of the Passover ever since.

When morning came, the Egyptians were wild with grief—practically ready to *push* the Hebrews out of the country. So the great movement called the Exodus began. (Exodus 5:1—12:42)

The most direct route from Egypt to Canaan would have been along the coast, but God had told Moses to bring the Israelites back to Mount Sinai where He had first spoken to Moses. There he would bind them into a real nation. To pass the holy mountain, Moses had to lead the people eastward, then south. A jutting arm of the Red Sea blocked their path, and as they started circling around this body of water, they heard the Egyptians coming after them. They turned and saw that Pharaoh had again changed his mind and sent his army to bring them back!

The people cried out to Moses, "Is it because there are no graves in Egypt that you have taken us away to die in the wilderness? What have you done to us, in bringing us out of Egypt?" They had not been happy as slaves, but they had felt safer than they did now!

But Moses said, "Fear not, stand firm, and see the salvation of the LORD, which he will work for you today." By now, Moses was radiant and steady. Even as he spoke, the sky began to change. A great cloud massed itself behind the Israelites so that the Egyptian army could not see them. Then a great wind rose, a strong wind which blew all night

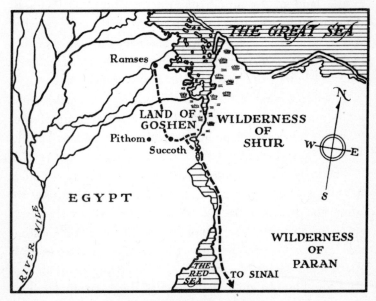

THE ESCAPE FROM EGYPT

and drove the sea back until there was dry land in front of the Israelites. Moses said, "Go," and the Israelites crossed over on dry land, "the waters being a wall to them on their right hand and on their left."

The Egyptians began to follow. Suddenly the wind dropped, the waters fell back in place. The Hebrews had reached the other side. The Egyptians never did. "Thus the LORD saved Israel that day from the land of the Egyptians . . . and the people feared the LORD; and they believed in the LORD and in his servant Moses." (Exodus 14)

## CHAPTER 10:

### BUILDING THE NATION

THE mixed multitude coming out of Egypt was not ready to colonize a new land. They had no feeling of being a nation. For this Moses had to prepare them. He began by reminding them that their faith was the faith of their fathers—of Abraham and Isaac and Jacob, to whom God had made a promise which was going to be fulfilled.

The journey to Mount Sinai probably took much longer than Moses expected. How slowly flocks and herds traveled, and how hard it was to find food and water for so many people and animals! However, the crossing of the Red Sea was but the first of a series of wonderful providences by which God made it plain to His people that He was not going to desert them. (Exodus 16)

When the Hebrews reached Mount Sinai, their life as a nation began. Before this, God had made covenants with individuals—Abraham, Isaac, Jacob. Now God made a covenant with the Israelites *as a people*.

It was very solemnly carried out. Moses, first of all, built a great altar of stone. He set up twelve big stones, one for each of the tribes of Israel. Then he sent young men to gather together sufficient animals from the flocks to make a great sacrifice. When they made a sacrifice, the Hebrews always cut the animal's throat and caught the blood in a basin. Half of the blood was poured over the altar which they had built in honor of God. The rest of the blood was sprinkled over the people. The important symbolism here is that the sacrificial blood was *divided* between God and the people, bringing them together into covenant. Moses told the people that they were a nation chosen out of all the tribes of the world to worship God and to live for His service.

Then God gave Moses "The Ten Words," or the "Decalogue." We call them the Ten Commandments. They are in our Prayer Book, which describes them as "the same which God spake to Moses on Mount Sinai." The Ten Words are not a legal code but a surrender of man to the Divine. The first "words" mean: "Accept God as He is—not as unbelievers describe Him, not as you would like Him to be, not even as you can most easily imagine Him—but as He *is*." Remember, the name Jehovah really means, "I am that which (who) I am." Behind the Sabbath law lies the fact that man's whole life is God's. Setting apart one day for worship is a recognition of this truth. It is in line with the old custom of offering God the first fruits of the land. "All things come of thee, O LORD, and of thine own have we given thee." It is man's forgetfulness of this fact that makes him ungenerous to God.

In the second group of "words," man is asked to honor his parents. Obedience to this commandment expresses

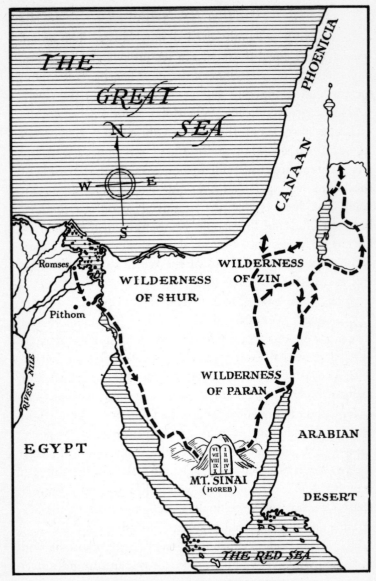

WANDERING IN THE WILDERNESS

acceptance of God's way of passing on the gift of life through generations.

The remaining "words" are the foundations of all law and order, of all social life. Without these foundations no nation can be great. There must be safeguards for life, marriage, property; there must be guarantees of truth in contracts and compacts.

Some ask why covetousness or envy is given such a detailed and lengthy definition. At first glance, envy seems so much less wicked than murder. But is it? The Epistle of St. James asks, "What causes wars, and what causes fightings among you? Is it not your passions that are at war in your members?" (4:1) Desire comes first, then inner conflict, then the outward act—the sins referred to in commandments six, seven, eight, and nine. Envy is the destruction of all that we mean by *community*.

When Moses had read the commandments to the people, he asked, "Will you accept these commandments?"

The people said, "What God has bidden us to do, we will do." (Exodus 19 and 20)

When you think of Moses leading and educating the Hebrews, do not picture him as some of the old painters did, with rod in hand, wild hair blowing about his stern and forbidding face, long horns of light standing out from his forehead. The Moses who was sent to save his people was the man who shared with them all the hardships of the way. He wasn't carried before them in a sedan chair by a troop of slaves. He knew human weakness in himself and could pardon it in others. He knew that only by going all the way *together* could the Israelites ever reach the fords of Jordan.

After the covenant was made, Moses and one companion, Joshua, went up on Mount Sinai. There Moses held what might be called a retreat. He needed to be alone with God so that, through prayer and meditation, he could gather strength for the hard work ahead. Imagine being faced with the job of leading a disorganized multitude of slaves just out of captivity, unused to working together or to doing anything on principle!

While Moses was on Mount Sinai, discontent again flared among the Hebrews. In Egypt they had become used to seeing people bow to idols of wood or stone or metal. Now they, too, wanted a god they could *see*.

Moses' brother Aaron, who had been left in charge, collected gold from the people and used it to make a golden calf for them to worship. When Moses came down from the mountain, carrying in his hands the stone tablets on which the commandments were written, he saw his people bowing down and dancing around the golden calf. He was appalled, and threw the stone tablets to the ground, breaking them to bits. Aaron was asked to account for his act, and the people had to undergo a severe punishment. (Exodus 32)

But God did not undo the covenant. In spite of the way the people had behaved, they were still to be His people. More than that, God encouraged Moses, telling him, "My presence will go with you and I will give you rest," a wonderful promise which referred also to the people.

Moses and the people needed God's comfort because they were not to come out of the wilderness for a long time—forty years by the usual reckoning. All this time God directed and protected them, guiding them with a cloud by day and at night giving them a light in the sky to follow. (Numbers 9:15–22) When they ran short of water or food, God showed Moses how to get it. (Exodus 16:11–15; 17:6)

The first time the Hebrews reached the border of the Holy Land, Moses sent twelve spies in to find out what the country was like. The spies reported that the land was fertile; it could grow anything. To prove that claim, they brought back a bunch of grapes so large it took two men to carry it. But the spies warned, "We came to the land to which you sent us; it flows with milk and honey, and this is its fruit. Yet the people who dwell in the land are strong, and the cities are fortified and very large. . . ." (Numbers 13:27–28)

At this, the Israelites began weeping and wailing again. They even said, "Let us go back to Egypt." Moses knew they did not really mean this, and he asked God to forgive them their lack of faith. But God ordered Moses to turn around and "set out for the wilderness by the way to the Red Sea"! It may seem that God was punishing the Hebrews by compelling them to wander in the wilderness for many more years, but He knew they had not learned to keep the law or to work together, so it was not yet time for them to enter the Promised Land.

It was in the wilderness that the Israelites began to hold their first services of worship. Moses had taught them to make a tabernacle or tent which could be folded up and carried with them. Inside the tabernacle was the Holy Ark, a box containing holy objects, among them a second set of stone tablets which Moses made to replace the ones he had broken. Whenever the people stopped and settled somewhere for a few days, they set up the tabernacle, placed the Ark within, and held worship services. Moses spent much time praying and meditating in the tabernacle. He got such comfort and strength from the experience that when he came out of the door of the tent it seemed to the people that his face was shining bright. They could hardly bear to look at him. So Moses veiled his face until the glory faded. The Bible description of Moses' bright face is there to tell us what a wonderful encouragement contact with God is. (Exodus 25–26; 33–34)

But Moses was not excused from trial and temptation. Once God said to him, "How long will this people despise me? And how long will they not believe in me, in spite of all the signs which I have wrought among them? I will strike them with the pestilence and disinherit them, and I will make of you a nation greater and mightier than they." (Numbers 14:11–12)

But Moses prayed for the people and said, "Pardon the iniquity of this people, I pray thee, according to the greatness of thy steadfast love, and according as thou hast forgiven this people, from Egypt even until now." (Numbers 14:19) That answer pleased God, because it showed how much Moses loved his people.

Moses continued to lead the Hebrews with love and patience until God called him to the top of Mount Pisgah, which is opposite Jericho, and showed him the Promised Land stretching out below.

"And the LORD said to him, 'This is the land of which I swore to Abraham, to Isaac, and to Jacob, "I will give it to your descendants." I have let you see it with your eyes, but you shall not go over there.' So Moses the servant of the Lord died there in the land of Moab, according to the word of the Lord, and he buried him in the valley in the land of Moab opposite Beth-peor; but no man knows the place of his burial to this day. Moses was a hundred and twenty years old when he died; his eye was not dim, nor his natural force abated. And the people of Israel wept for Moses in the plains of Moab thirty days; then the days of weeping and mourning for Moses were ended.

"And Joshua the son of Nun was full of the spirit of wisdom, for Moses had laid his hands upon him; so the people of Israel obeyed him, and did as the Lord had commanded Moses. And there has not arisen a prophet since in Israel like Moses, whom the Lord knew face to face." (Deuteronomy 34:4–10)

## CHAPTER II:

### ENTERING THE PROMISED LAND

THE last chapter was about the wanderings of the Hebrew people and how at last they reached a place on the east bank of the river Jordan, where it was possible to cross into Canaan. They had approached in a roundabout way and had taken possession of this eastern area so that when they did settle in Palestine they would not be threatened by enemies coming across the river to attack them.

Look at the map on page 66. Notice the long strip of seacoast on the west, and the river Jordan, east of center, running straight down from the mountains of Lebanon at the top of the map to the Dead Sea at the bottom.

The Jordan is a deep and rapid river, closed in almost all the way by chalky cliffs. Here and there the cliffs level down, forming natural fords where it is possible to cross. It was at such a place that the Hebrews now found themselves, just north of the Dead Sea and opposite the city of

Jericho. Through the years, wild tribes had occasionally crossed the river at this point to attack Jericho. But these raiders had come lightly armed, usually on fast horses. They had never been encumbered with old men, women, and children, or with flocks and herds of sheep, goats, and oxen, as the Hebrews were. Even with these handicaps, the people might not have been so frightened at the thought of trying to capture Jericho if Moses had been leading them.

All through the wilderness they had had one leader, Moses. All through those forty years of wandering, they had depended on him. He was always the same, whether they cursed him or whether they blessed him; he was always there, pointing the way; and only once during the whole journey had he lost his temper with them. (That seems the greatest miracle of all.) They knew he loved them, and they knew he was living only for God and for them. Now he was dead! How could they possibly do without him at this crucial time?

But, of course, Moses had anticipated this situation. He knew it must be, and he had been preparing another man to take his place. That man was Joshua. He was not related to Moses. He belonged to the tribe of Ephraim, whereas Moses, as far as we know, was a Levite. Joshua was a young man when they started, and Moses trained him not only in leadership but also in trust in God.

Just notice this man's name, for it is interesting. He had been called Hoshea at the beginning, but Moses changed his name to Joshua. Hoshea means "Salvation," but Joshua means "the LORD is salvation." That was the best kind of name to give a man who had a big task and needed all the help that God could give him.

Think of Joshua for a moment, and what he would have seen as he stood on a little hill looking across the Jordan toward the city he must conquer before the Israelites could go on. First of all, he would have seen a plain about fourteen miles wide and, snaking through the middle of it, a long green streak of trees which hid the river from sight but marked its course. Beyond the river, in the far corner of the plain, stood the city of Jericho, circled around by palm trees and a stream of fresh water. How pleasant it must have looked to a man just off the desert. But behind Jericho rose a solid wall of mountains, about three thousand feet high. Beyond these mountains was the Promised Land.

As Joshua stood there, surveying the land, thinking of what he had to do, his first great encouragement came. He

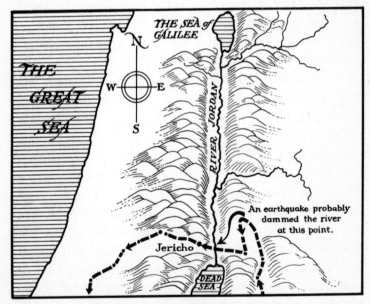

ENTERING THE PROMISED LAND

heard a voice in his heart. As clearly as God had spoken to Moses or Abraham, He now said to Joshua, "No man shall be able to stand before you all the days of your life; as I was with Moses, so I will be with you; I will not fail you or forsake you. Be strong and of good courage; for you shall cause this people to inherit the land which I swore to their fathers to give them." Then Joshua realized that if God plans work for His people, He sees it through with them, even though the task seems to call for a miracle. (Joshua 1:5)

What is a miracle anyhow? It is not something you can plan. It just happens. Sometimes it is an astonishing happening. More often it is an ordinary incident which turns out in a wonderful way. For example, it is a miracle if you go down one street and get home quite safely, whereas you could have taken another street and been killed by a falling chimney. It's a miracle on God's side. He saved you just as surely as if he had stopped the chimney in the air. And as far as we can see, that is the way that God most often works. He uses the powers of nature more often than He sets them aside. A miracle may be a wonderful thing in itself, or it may be a thing which is quite ordinary which God causes to turn out in a wonderful way. In either case, it calls for faith that God, not man, rules the world. The result is that the human mind realizes God is at work and is filled with wonder and thankfulness that it should be so.

Now a lot of things had happened in the desert journeys that seemed to the people of Israel like miracles. There was the crossing of the Red Sea to begin with. In just what kind of way it was a miracle we can't be certain, but it was miracle enough that they could get across where they did. Then, too, there was the wonder that all through the wanderings in the wilderness, the Israelites never failed to have food and drink. They would always find it—sometimes in an unexpected way—and they got the feeling by degrees that there was a power behind them that helped them do what they never could have done alone. They felt that something was happening that they never could have managed themselves. At any rate, the best of them felt this way—Joshua among them. Some of the Israelites, of course, grumbled and complained as people always will, but Joshua had become more and more sure of God.

Still, Joshua didn't sit down and wait for a miracle to take place. He did what any good commander would do, what Moses had done once before. He sent scouts across the river to see if the people of Jericho were making preparations against attack. The scouts came back and said that the people were afraid but were trusting the city's mighty walls. Although the Bible doesn't say so, Joshua must have sent scouts up and down the river on the east side, too. Meanwhile he organized the Israelites into groups so that when it came time to cross, there would be no confusion or delay. Then, to remind the people that this was a religious enterprise, he instructed the priests to lead the crossing. He told them to take the Holy Ark and carry it to the edge of the water, where they were to wait for the word to advance. The Ark, a gilded chest, was considered so holy that no one dared touch it. It was supplied with corner rings through which were thrust gilded poles for the priests to carry on their shoulders.

The people assembled behind the priests with the Ark.

Suddenly, as they stood waiting for Joshua's command, the earth began to tremble and shake. Whether or not the Hebrews knew that earthquakes were common in this area, they must have had to call up all their faith to hold their stand as the earth shook under their feet. Psalm 114 gives us an idea of what they must have thought.

> When Israel went forth from Egypt,
>   the house of Jacob from a people
>     of strange language,
> Judah became his sanctuary,
>   Israel his domination.
>
> The sea looked and fled,
>   Jordan turned back.
> The mountains skipped like rams,
>   the hills like lambs.
>
> What ails you, O sea, that you flee?
>   O Jordan, that you turn back?
> O mountains, that you skip like rams?
>   O hills, like lambs?
>
> Tremble, O earth, at the presence of
>   the LORD,
> at the presence of the God of Jacob ...

We can imagine the Hebrews waiting to see what would happen next, and perhaps the scouts running down from the north, crying, "The river banks are falling in. The whole stream is dammed up north of us." Very soon the people saw the shallow water of the ford begin to sink lower and lower and drain away into the Dead Sea. Now only a few inches of water covered the river bottom. Joshua gave the word. The priests carried the Ark to the center of the river bed and waited there until all the people had passed over to the other side. They were now on the very shore of the Promised Land.

Thus had God done. It was just as great a miracle as if He had dried up the water without any earthquake at all. (Joshua 2 and 3)

However, this was only the beginning. There was still Jericho to be taken. Joshua knew exactly what he was doing. There was not going to be a great battle or anything of that kind. It was going to be a great religious ceremony. According to Jewish law, man is to offer God the first fruits of every undertaking: the first lamb, kid, or calf slaughtered, the first sheaves of grain gathered from the field, the first fruit picked from the orchard. Joshua thought about this first city to be taken in Canaan, and decided that it should be an offering to God. He instructed the people to form a circle around the city. The fighting men were to form a long procession led by seven priests carrying the Ark and blowing rams'-horn trumpets. This procession was to march around Jericho every day for six days, the priests blowing the trumpets but no one else making a sound. On the seventh day, the procession was to go around the city seven times; and when Joshua gave the signal, all the people were to give one mighty shout. In a way, it was a war of nerves, with the people inside Jericho getting more and more jumpy waiting for an attack.

And the story, as the Bible tells it, is that when the people shouted, the walls of Jericho fell, and the Israelites had only to enter the city. Maybe there was another earthquake. We don't know, but a professor who excavated Jericho a few years ago says the walls fell *outward*, and whatever the reason, the city fell without a battle.[1]

Only one family in Jericho was spared—the family of Rahab, a woman who had helped Joshua's spies avoid capture. Rahab later married an Israelite, and her name appears in the first chapter of the Gospel According to St. Matthew in the geneology of Jesus. (Joshua 6:17–19)

Joshua was a great military commander, but he was something more, as the following stories show. Before the Israelites entered Jericho, Joshua made an announcement forbidding any of them to take plunder. An Israelite named Achan disobeyed. He took a wedge of silver, a wedge of gold, and an embroidered cloak, and hid them in his tent. His crime was discovered by casting lots, and he was brought before Joshua. You can imagine how he fell in a kind of huddled heap at the feet of the great leader.

Pardon, of course, was impossible. Achan must die, because he had brought a curse on the whole people. One might expect to hear a great commander like Joshua sternly ordering, "Carry him away to the place of stoning." But no, Joshua looked pityingly on the man and said, "My son, give glory to the Lord God of Israel, and render praise to him; and tell me now what you have done; do not hide it from me."

Achan said, "Of a truth I have sinned against the Lord God of Israel." The Jewish rabbis of a later date said that, by his confession of his sin and his penitence before his execution, though he was cast out from the convocation of

---

[1] *The National Geographic* Magazine, December, 1953, "Jericho Gives Up Its Secrets."

Israel on earth, Achan obtained a place in the world to come. (Joshua 7:19–20)

The other story about Joshua happened when he was one hundred and ten years old. At this time, he divided the land among the tribes, called them all together, and reminded them that without the help of God they could never have come into Canaan or conquered it. He told them quite frankly that the God of Israel, Jehovah, was a hard God to serve. He was not like those Canaanite gods that only wanted a few sacrifices. Jehovah must be served in sincerity and in truth with a whole heart. He challenged the tribes to choose between this God who had done so much for them and the easy-to-please idols of the heathen. Then Joshua drew himself up to his full height and said, "As for me and my house, we will serve the LORD." So he died and passed on his name through the generations. (Joshua 24:15)

The Israelites often gave the names of their great men to their children, just as we do. The name Joshua was a great name for centuries after that. About a thousand years later, a great conqueror named Alexander came into Egypt and the western part of Asia, and the people there had to change their language. In that section of the land the Bible of the Jews had to be changed into Greek, and all the names, when put into Greek letters, took a different kind of sound. What happened to the name Joshua? It changed into what St. Paul calls "the name that is above every name," *Jesus*.

In the first chapter of St. Matthew we read that the angel came to Joseph and spoke about the Holy Child that was to be born. The angel said, "You shall call His name

Jesus, for He will save His people from their sins." Joseph and Mary knew perfectly well that he was referring to Joshua, whose name meant "the LORD is salvation." Jesus came to save His people from an enemy more terrible than the Egyptians. He came to lead them to a land more happy than Canaan. He came in answer to a promise. The story of Joshua is one of the important stages in the fulfillment of this promise.

# CHAPTER 12:

## SAMSON

IT IS an undoubted fact of history that some time between the thirteenth and twelfth centuries before our Lord's coming, a strange people came to live in the land of Palestine, on the east coast of the Mediterranean, between Mount Carmel and the Egyptian border. These people were the Philistines, for whom Palestine was eventually named.

To find out about the Philistines, we must go back to events which a hundred years ago were not thought of as history at all, but as Greek fairy tales, preserved through the centuries in songs once sung at festivals in honor of the gods. Many of these songs were about a war between the Greeks on one side and the Trojans, the most important people of Asia Minor, on the other—a war some say was fought over a woman, the famous Helen of Troy. In the end, the Greeks won the war, and the city of Troy was destroyed. All this, if it ever happened, was thought to have occurred somewhere in the thirteenth century B.C.

74

Then in the year A.D. 1878, a patient German scholar went to Asia Minor and dug down in the place where Troy was supposed, by legend, to have been. He found not one, but nine cities, each built on the ruins of the last! After that discovery, the work of excavation went ahead all over the Near East.

There are monuments in Egypt which show pictures of a great number of people traveling down the coast from Asia Minor. They are probably the remains of tribes who had been mixed up with one side or other in the war round Troy. Down the coast they came, looking for new homes, bringing their women and children in queer, little-wheeled wagons. These were the Philistines. They weren't a bit like the Egyptians or the Hebrews. They had long oval faces and fine features, which show that they belonged to the Aegean race, a race which takes its name from the Aegean Sea washing the coast of Greece. The men were well armed and wore high-plumed helmets. They were remnants of a great early civilization which at that time seemed to be losing its place in the Mediterranean world. Their ships followed them along the coast.

The Philistines tried to find a place for themselves in Egypt, but Ramses III, king of Egypt, was not to be imposed on. There were fierce land and sea battles. In one picture, which shows a sea battle, the men with plumed helmets are falling into the sea in great numbers before the attacks of the Egyptians.

But it was not a complete massacre. Ramses stopped the Philistines from entering Egypt, but, with or without his permission, they stayed just beyond his northern border on

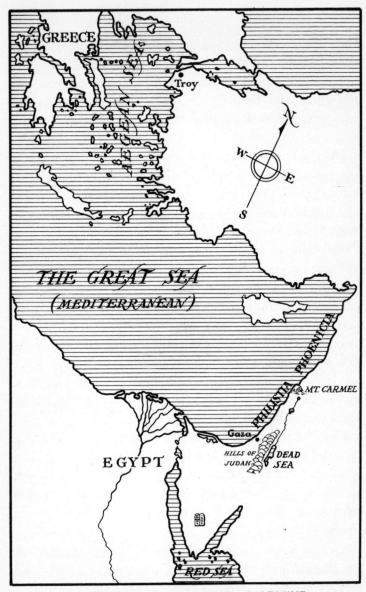

LAND OF THE PHILISTINES—PALESTINE

a stretch of coast close to lands occupied by the Hebrews coming in from the east.

The first Hebrew tribe the Philistines clashed with was the tribe of Simeon, which had never been well established and now disappeared entirely. Next the Philistines encountered the little tribe of Dan. Not strong enough to drive off the Philistines, the Danites still maintained an attitude of protest.

One of the Danites was named Samson. His story is the story of a lost opportunity, a mission only partially fulfilled in death.

The Danite Samson was a legendary hero, one of many who are supposed to have lived at this time when "there was no king in Israel, and every man did what was right in his own eyes." The tales of some of these heroes really have historical foundations, although they are hard to verify. But even in the case of stories which cannot be proved, it is important to recognize the reason why such heroes were held in high honor.

Because of the Epistle to the Hebrews, we know what Jews living at the time of Jesus thought about the early records of their heroes. They thought these scriptures were written for our learning—not just to please and entertain us, but to show the real meaning of God's help to their fathers.

Samson's birth had been announced to his parents by an angel who told them that the coming child should be dedicated to Jehovah. He was to be a Nazirite. This meant that he took vows to serve God. The Nazirites were not a religious order: they were free to marry, and they were not banded together in groups. But each was dedicated to serve God individually, holding himself ready for God's call. Nazirites never drank wine or liquor or cut their hair.

In spite of this solemn preparation, Samson grew up more like a playboy than like a servant of God. He made friends with his country's enemies and ignored his father's wishes by marrying a Philistine.

The most remarkable thing about Samson was his great strength. It was the marvel of the countryside, and the Philistines, especially, wanted to know the secret of it. Samson himself thought his strength was connected with his uncut hair; that it was a kind of magic power he could do what he wanted with. He had to learn that his strength was really the gift of God and as such was at God's disposal.

Because Samson was the Danites' great champion, the Philistines bent every effort to capture him. Finally, they went to Delilah, Samson's Philistine wife. "Entice him," they said, "and see wherein his great strength lies, and by what means we may overpower him, that we may bind him to subdue him; [do this] and we will each give you eleven hundred pieces of silver."

When Delilah begged Samson to tell her wherein his strength lay and how he might be bound and subdued, Samson made up a story about special rope being needed. That night as he slept, Delilah got the Philistines to tie Samson with the kind of rope he had specified. But Samson snapped the ropes like thread.

Three times Delilah asked Samson to tell her his secret. Three times Samson invented an answer. Then Delilah said,

"How can you say, 'I love you,' when your heart is not with me? You have mocked me these three times, and you have not told me wherein your great strength lies." She continued to beg and cry, and finally Samson gave in.

"A razor has never come upon my head," he said. "If I be shaved, then my strength will leave me, and I shall become weak, and be like any other man." Delilah promptly relayed *this* information to the Philistines. Then she got Samson to sleep with his head on her knees; and while he slept, she let a man shave off his hair. The she cried, "The Philistines are upon you, Samson!"

"And he woke from his sleep, and said, 'I will go out as at other times, and shake myself free.' "

But the Bible says, "He did not know that the LORD had left him."

Samson was captured by the Philistines who gouged out his eyes and took him away to prison in the city of Gaza. In prison the hair of his head began to grow. And, as his later words and deeds show, something else began to grow in Samson's heart and conscience: a humility and sense of consecration which had never been his before.

In time, a festival was held at Gaza. The chief men of the city, their wives and families as well as townspeople of lesser rank, gathered at a lofty temple which had a wide doorway supported by two massive pillars. Someone got the idea that it might be amusing to exhibit the prize captive and make fun of him.

As he was brought in from the prison, Samson felt his old strength rising up in him, and he was filled with the wild hope that he might be able in this one day to atone for his broken vow and his wasted life. He began by stretching his arms a little to amuse the people and yet give them no idea of what was in his mind.

Samson was led between the pillars in the doorway where everyone could see him. "The house was full of men and women; all the lords of the Philistines were there, and on the roof there were about three thousand men and women, who looked on . . ." Samson said to the boy who held his hand, "Let me feel the pillars on which the house rests, that I may lean against them."

Suddenly he cried, "O Lord God, remember me, I pray thee, and strengthen me, I pray thee, only this once, O God." At the same moment, he caught hold of the pillars, one with his right hand, the other with his left, and he pushed outward with all his might. "Let me die with the Philistines," he said, and the roof came crashing down upon them all. (Judges 13–16)

The poet Milton imagines Samson's father saying:

> Living or dying, thou hast fulfilled thy work for
>     which thou wast foretold to Israel.
> Samson has quit himself like Samson—no time for
>     lamentations now.[1]

SUGGESTIONS FOR FURTHER READING: Judges 6–8, the story of Gideon; Ruth 1–4, the story of Ruth.

---

[1]John Milton, *Samson Agonistes*.

## CHAPTER 13:

### SAMUEL

AFTER the battle of Jericho, the sacred Ark was set up in a
tabernacle or holy tent at Shiloh, near the shrine of Bethel
where Jacob had once seen the angels going up and down
the ladder to heaven. Later, regular services were held at
Shiloh, led by an old priest, Eli, a descendant of Moses'
brother, Aaron. Eli seemed to have had a hereditary right
to be in charge of the tent of worship, and it was taken for
granted that his sons would succeed him, although they
were known to be wicked and unfit for the office.

At this point we hear of a man named Elkanah coming
up to the tabernacle for worship. Elkanah had two wives,
but Hannah, the one he loved the better, had no children.
Hannah came to the tabernacle with her husband to pray
for a child. When Eli saw her weeping, he gave her hope
that God would answer her prayer. In gratitude Hannah
promised that if God blessed her with a son, she would
offer the child to Him for service in the sanctuary.

God answered Hannah's prayer and sent her a son, whom she called Samuel. The hymn of thanksgiving she sang when he was born reminds us of the Virgin Mary's song, which we call the Magnificat. When St. Luke wrote the story of the birth of Jesus, he must have remembered Samuel's story, for he said, "And Jesus increased in wisdom and in stature, and in favor with God and man." Similar words are spoken of Samuel. (I Samuel 1)

As a boy, Samuel served as an acolyte in the holy tent. One night he heard the voice of God calling him by name, "Samuel! Samuel!" Samuel answered as Eli had taught him to answer: "Speak, Lord, for thy servant hears." But it was a terrible message Samuel was given to pass on to old Eli, and it must have been very hard to deliver. Samuel was told to tell Eli that his two sons had brought a curse upon themselves, and that their descendants would never again be allowed to serve in the house of the Lord.

Eli knew that his sons were wicked, and he said, "It *is* the Lord; let him do what seems good to him."

Word soon got around that the voice of the Lord had been heard in the tabernacle. "Who heard him?" the people must have asked. And Eli must have answered that it was Samuel who had heard God. Gradually the people became convinced that young Samuel was a prophet of the Lord. (I Samuel 3)

Being a prophet often has very little to do with talking about the future. A prophet is one who speaks out plainly. What he says has to do, for the most part, with what is happening now. From time to time in history there have been court prophets appointed by kings to say just what the kings wanted. There have also been other men called "seers," who for a small fee would tell you where to find lost things; they would even curse your enemies for you. Some of them went into trances and whirled around like the dervishes in Moslem lands. But none of these, of course, was honored like a true prophet.

Now Samuel was, after Moses, the first of the true prophets of whom we know anything. A true prophet of the LORD is a man who from his early youth has led a life of prayer and communion with God, so that as time goes on he sees the world and everything in it almost as God sees it. He even understands God's mind a little and can deliver messages from God to men, even to kings and priests—if he is willing to risk being an unwelcome messenger.

After Samuel delivered his unwelcome message to Eli, his activities are not reported in detail again until the Israelites and the Philistines waged full-scale war against each other. When the battle began to go against the Israelites, they sent a message to Shiloh asking for the Holy Ark to be brought to the battlefield. It was not a sin to take the Ark to a battle. Ever since Moses had built it, the Ark had gone before the Israelites into their adventures. The Holy Ark at the head of the marching host was a reminder of God's promise to Moses: "My presence will go with you, and I will give you rest." Breaking camp in the morning, Moses would cry, "Arise, O LORD, and let thy enemies be scattered." The priests would take up the Holy Ark, and the journey would continue. At night, Moses would say, "Return, O LORD, to the ten thousand thousands of Israel." (Numbers 10:35–36)

Some people have the idea that the Israelites thought

God lived inside the Ark. Hebrew scholars say that this was never the case. The Ark was no idol. It was not shaped like any animal, plant, or bird. It was simply a rectangular chest. On its gold cover stood two cherubs with out-stretched wings. In the Bible, cherubs are not curly-haired babies with wings at the backs of their necks. They are more like great eagles or the winged lions on Assyrian monuments. The wings of the cherubs on the Ark joined in front forming a throne. So the Ark was sometimes called the Throne of God. The Ark was also called the Ark of Witness, because it housed the stone tablets on which the Ten Commandments were written.

Eli still served as chief priest at Shiloh, and despite God's warning, and his own misgivings, he let his sons continue as priests in the holy tent. Although it was proper and tradi-tional for the Israelites to send for the Ark upon this occa-sion, they should not have looked on it as a guarantee of victory, and this is what Eli allowed them to do. Now the most dreadful thing happened that could happen: the Ark was seized by their enemies!

Why was it that, on the field of battle, the Ark was cap-tured by the enemy? And why was there no victory if the Ark was so holy? The answer isn't far to seek. Who car-ried the Ark? It was those two evil sons of Eli. They held the long poles which carried the Ark, and it was because *their* hands were on the poles that the Ark was forsaken, as it were, by God and carried away by the enemy. This loss was so dreadful for all the people that the messenger came running as quickly as possible to Eli, who was at Shiloh, to say that his two sons were killed and the Ark was taken. (I Samuel 4)

Eli died of shock when the news of his sons' deaths was brought to him. It was Samuel who took over the task of helping the people through the hard times that followed. The Philistines did not keep the Ark. It seemed to them that the Ark brought them nothing but bad luck, and they sent it back of their own accord. For some reason, however, it was not replaced in the tabernacle at Shiloh. In fact, it seems likely that Shiloh itself was destroyed by the Philistines. The Ark was sent to a private house, and there it remained until the time of David. (I Samuel 6–7)

Samuel was neither a priest nor a king, but he was a judge, and in his role of judge he had great authority. He traveled from place to place, settling disputes. The people loved and admired Samuel, but as the Philistines began to seize more and more of their country, the Israelites began to wish for a fierce and warlike king. "Give us a king to lead us to battle," they said.

Samuel wondered if the people ought to have a king, but he did not take it upon himself to decide. He waited for God to direct him. Finally God assured Samuel that there was to be a king and how he was to be recognized and anointed. (I Samuel 8)

## CHAPTER 14:

### KING SAUL

SAUL was a handsome young farmer from the tribe of Benjamin. He had come to Samuel's city to look for some donkeys his father had lost. Except that he stood head and shoulders above everyone else, Saul did not look like a king, but when Samuel saw him coming, he knew at once that this was the man God had asked him to anoint.

At Samuel's invitation, Saul attended a banquet and spent the night in the city. In the morning, Samuel accompanied Saul to the outskirts of town. There he drew him aside and performed the anointing ceremony, saying, "Has not the LORD anointed you to be prince over his people Israel?"

A few days later, Samuel called the tribes together to hold an election. Elections in those days were decided by the casting of lots. The people thought that by casting lots they put the choice in God's hands. In this election, Saul was chosen. He was so modest and shy that, when the people went to tell him he had been elected, they could not find him. He was hiding among the baggage. "Then they ran and fetched him from there . . . and Samuel said to the people, 'Do you see him whom the LORD has chosen? There is none like him among all the people.' And all the people shouted, 'Long live the king!'"

Samuel explained the rights and duties of kingship and wrote them in a book. Then he sent everyone away. Saul went back to his father's farm to wait until he was needed.

He did not have to wait long. The city of Jabesh on the far side of the Jordan fell under siege. If the people of the city did not have help within three or four days, they would have to give themselves up to the Ammonites who had threatened to enslave them and to put out the right eye of every captive they took. Hearing that there was a new king, the inhabitants of Jabesh sent a desperate message to him.

Saul conscripted a civilian army, broke the siege of Jabesh, and saved the inhabitants. Now all the people of Israel were ready to follow him.

Saul was a brave fighter and a good military strategist. Under his leadership the Israelites carried out a series of successful raids and skirmishes against the Philistines. But, unfortunately, Saul was not working out his kingship according to Samuel's direction. Samuel had told Saul that the king of Israel was not to be an absolute monarch, planning everything to please himself. The king of Israel was to be a new kind of king—one who asked God's advice and considered the will and welfare of the people.

But the people of Israel had said, "Give us a king like the kings of other nations," and that was exactly the kind of king Saul wanted to be. As long as he could have everything his own way, he did not mind paying God a few sacrifices afterward. He did not like to ask God what *God* wanted done, but he did not mind asking God to help Saul do what *Saul* wanted. (It is interesting to compare the kings of Hebrew history. Many were like Saul, but a few were like David, a model king in that he usually tried to find out God's plan and follow it.)

At last Samuel had to tell Saul that his kingdom would not continue; that the LORD had sought out a man after His own heart and appointed him to be prince over the people.

By this time, Saul was very hard to live with. He had fits of melancholy when he buried himself in his tent and refused to speak to anyone. At one of these times, a friend suggested that music might help. Someone remembered a young man who played the harp and had a good singing voice. According to one Bible account, this was David. So David entered history—a "man of good presence" brought to King Saul's tent to comfort him with music. He played for Saul, and for a while the music seemed to help. But before long something else also happened to rouse Saul. (I Samuel 16:18)

For some time the Philistines had been quiet. Now they began to attack. Both sides sensed that a great battle was in the offing. The Israelites under Saul called up every available man. At last the two armies faced each other across the valley of Elah. The bronze armor, spears, and shields of the Philistines glistened in the sun.

Suddenly out from the Philistine line strode a huge man wearing a crested helmet and a coat of mail. A bronze javelin was slung between his shoulders, and the spear he carried was long and heavy. "Choose a man for yourselves," the big man shouted to the ranks of Israel, "and let him come down to me. If he is able to fight with me and kill me, then we will be your servants; but if I prevail against him and kill him, then you shall be our servants and serve us."

Day after day Goliath shouted his challenge and got no answer. Then, as it happened, David was sent to the battle-field with food for his soldier brothers. He heard the giant's challenge, and he went to King Saul and said that he would like to fight Goliath if Saul would give him permission.

Saul considered this a fantastic request, but he said, "Go, and the LORD be with you!" Then he offered David his helmet, a coat of mail, a sword, and a spear.

David tried them on, but he said, "I am not used to them." Instead, he decided to use the sling and stone with which he protected himself and his sheep from bears and lions. "The LORD who delivered me from the paw of the lion and from the paw of the bear will deliver me from the hand of this Philistine," he said. And he went to the brook, chose five smooth stones, and put them in his shepherd's bag. So the two met, the giant with his crested helmet and his sword and his spear and his mocking words; the young shepherd with his sling.

When Goliath saw David coming, he called out, "Am I a dog, that you come to me with sticks?"

David answered, "You come to me with a sword and with a spear and with a javelin; but I come to you in the name of the LORD of hosts, the God of the armies of Israel, whom you have defied. This day the LORD will deliver you into my hand."

"And David put his hand in his bag and took out a stone,

and slung it, and struck the Philistine on his forehead; the stone sank into his forehead, and he fell on his face to the ground." (I Samuel 17)

This story is symbolically true. It happened because a young man had faith in God and in the destiny of his people. David remembered that long ago God had promised Abraham, "Unto thy seed will I give this land." At the valley of Elah, the land was in danger of being lost. God saved it through David.

It would be wonderful if the story could end with everyone living happily ever after. The story doesn't end that way, because Saul grew jealous of David. Saul wanted the victory for himself—not for God. When the women of the cities of Israel turned out to give Saul and David a hero's welcome, they sang,

> "Saul has slain his thousands,
> And David his ten thousands."

Saul thought, "They have ascribed to David ten thousands, and to me they have ascribed [only] thousands; and what more can he have but the kingdom?"

It was not long before Saul tried to kill David, but David evaded Saul's spear. Actually, David was so well loved that Saul had some misgivings about killing him openly. So he pushed David into front-line positions where he might be killed by the Philistines. When this maneuver did not work, Saul tried to get his son and his servants to kill David.

Now Saul's son, Jonathan, was a true friend to David. The Bible says, "the soul of Jonathan was knit to the soul of David, and Jonathan loved him as his own soul." Jonathan warned David of Saul's plot. He also tried to talk to

Saul about David; but the more Jonathan defended David, the angrier Saul grew. Finally, in a towering rage, Saul hurled a spear at his own son. Then Jonathan knew that he and David could not continue to meet as friends.

They went to a secret place to say good-by. Jonathan might have gone with David, but he never seems to have doubted for a moment that his duty was to his father. Jonathan and David prayed together, "The LORD shall be between me and you, and between my descendants and your descendants, for ever." Then Jonathan returned to the city. This was no easy choice, because Saul was getting harder to live with all the time, and anyone could see that he was on the way to defeat and ruin which must destroy the whole family. But Jonathan was not thinking of himself. (I Samuel 20)

Neither was David putting himself first when the swift and silent movements which his manner of life required brought him upon Saul, asleep and helpless. David's friends urged him to revenge himself upon Saul. But David said, "The LORD forbid that I should . . . put forth my hand against him, seeing he is the LORD's anointed." A second time David spared Saul's life, taking only the king's spear which was planted in the ground by his side. In the morning, David shouted to Saul that he might send a messenger to get it.

David's generosity touched Saul's conscience, but only for a moment. Once Saul said to David, "You are more righteous than I; for you have repaid me good, whereas I have repaid you evil." Saul asked David to promise that he would not kill his descendants. David promised willingly. (I Samuel 24)

Time passed. David busied himself building up the guerrilla forces which would be needed in the future. The strip of land the Israelites still held grew narrower and narrower. At last the Philistines gathered to put the finishing touch on the remnants of Saul's army. In desperation, Saul considered calling on the God he had so long ignored. But how could he seek God? Samuel was dead. David was banished. Saul himself had killed all the priests in the city of Nob because they had once sheltered David. Like other desperate men before his time and after, Saul turned his thoughts to forbidden paths. He would try magic. He would consult the witch of Endor.

In an underground cave with a dim light hanging from the roof, an old woman crouches. Her cracked voice echoes through the hollows. "Whom shall I bring up for you?"

Saul remembers the friend and adviser of his youth. "Bring up Samuel for me."

There is a pause. The old woman says, "An old man is coming up; and he is wrapped in a robe."

It is Samuel, but he has no comfort to bring. He says to Saul, "Tomorrow you and your sons shall be with me; the LORD will give the army of Israel also into the hand of the Philistines."

The old woman looks around. Saul is stretched out on the floor in terror and despair. (I Samuel 28)

The next day the Philistines made their big push against Israel. Saul and his sons, his armor-bearer and all his men, died on Mount Gilboa.

The Philistines cut off Saul's head and carried it to one of their temples. They hung his body on the walls of Bethshan.

But in the midst of this cruelty, a debt of gratitude was paid. Across the Jordan from Bethshan lay Jabesh-gilead, the little city which Saul had saved in the bright days of his early kingship. When the men of Jabesh-gilead heard of Saul's fate, they made a night raid on Bethshan and brought Saul's body back to Jabesh-gilead for a burial with honor.

David remembered Saul's early triumphs, too, and wrote a beautiful lament for Saul and for Jonathan:

> Saul and Jonathan, beloved and lovely!
> In life and in death they were not divided;
> they were swifter than eagles,
> they were stronger than lions . . .
>
> How are the mighty fallen
> in the midst of the battle!
>
> Jonathan lies slain upon thy high places.
> I am distressed for you, my brother Jonathan;
> very pleasant have you been to me;
> your love to me was wonderful,
> passing the love of women.
>
> How are the mighty fallen,
> and the weapons of war perished!
>
> (II Samuel 1:23–27)

### CHAPTER 15:

### KING DAVID

DAVID was to become the first Hebrew king with fully constituted power. The wonderful account of his life which is given in the Second Book of Samuel is thought to be quite reliable. It is based on an ancient document called "David's Court Chronicle."

During Saul's lifetime, David and his men had moved from one secret stronghold to another, avoiding any direct clash with the Philistines or with Saul. One of the anecdotes preserved from this period gives us insight into the situation. We are told that once, while David was in hiding, he longed for a drink of water from the well that was by the gate of Bethlehem. Bethlehem had been his home, but now it was in the hands of the Philistines. Three of David's devoted followers, knowing his longing, broke through the Philistine lines at the peril of their lives. When they returned to David with the water, David would not drink it.

Instead he poured out the water as a sacrifice to God, something too precious to use. "Far be it from me, O Lord, that I should do this," he said. "Shall I drink the blood of the men who went at the risk of their lives?"

After the death of Saul and his three eldest sons on Mount Gilboa, David was able to come out of hiding and to try to pull together the scattered powers of Israel. Saul had left no son capable of taking his place. But then, he had left no kingdom to inherit! Saul's one remaining son, Ishbosheth, tried to set up a kingdom on the other side of the Jordan. At first he was assisted by Abner, his uncle. But Abner soon deserted his nephew and made peace with David. Ishbosheth doesn't seem to have been much of a man, and his friends, seeing that his cause was hopeless, eventually helped David by getting rid of him. (II Samuel 4)

David might have given Abner a place in his own army but for the vengefulness of Joab. Joab and Abishai were nephews of David and gave him loyal and devoted service all his life, even love of the kind rough men understand. But in this case they had a family account to settle. Sometime before, Abner and the younger brother of Joab and Abishai had met in a battle, and the young man had pursued Abner until Abner had killed him in self-defense. But the brothers of the slain man now wanted vengeance. They certainly were not going to allow Abner to have a place of respect in David's kingdom. So they satisfied both their grudge and their jealousy by killing Abner. This was only the beginning of David's displeasure with Joab. For years he was to be annoyed and enraged by his nephew, and yet Joab did things for David that had to be done. David could not have got along without his ruthless honesty and devotion. (II Samuel 2 and 4)

When David was anointed king and assumed leadership, he had many loyal followers but no land of his own. From this time on, David and his men won back the lost lands of Israel, step by step. Then they went on to conquer a much wider realm than that little country ever had included before, or has ever included again. (II Samuel 5:3–5)

The most thrilling point for the Israelites was the capture of Jerusalem. The city had never been taken from the Canaanites in all the years since the Hebrews first came into the land. Jerusalem was very strongly fortified by nature. Being built on a hill with rocky, precipitous sides, it could easily be defended. In fact, there was a saying, "The blind and the lame could hold Jerusalem against David or anybody." But David's nephew Joab climbed up through the underground tunnel that brought water to the city, and he and a few men were able to surprise the garrison from within. (II Samuel 5)

Jerusalem was not only a beautiful, strong city; it was also an ideal site for a new center of government. Establishing his capital in Jerusalem saved David from the jealousies and bickering that might have sprung up if he had chosen a capital in either the north or the south, or in any city that had formerly sought power.

More than this, Jerusalem gave David the opportunity of making a new center of worship for his people. His first great festival of thanksgiving was crowned by bringing up the Holy Ark from the private home where it had been kept ever since it was returned by the Philistines. David wanted to build a great temple to house the Ark and to be

DAVID'S KINGDOM

the national center of worship, but the prophet Nathan brought word from the LORD that it was not David, but his son who was to have the honor of building the temple.

David proved his devotion to the God of his fathers by his willingness to run the kingdom the way God wanted it run. Strong as he was, David accepted the fact that God's prophet must be his ruling partner. Saul had always refused to permit any such partnership. (II Samuel 7)

When David was securely established in power, he asked if any members of the house of Saul were left. If so, he wanted to show them kindness for the sake of Jonathan. Word was brought that one child remained, a lame boy, the son of Jonathan. David sent for him and gave to him the wealth that had been Saul's and made the boy a member of his own household. The memory of his friendship with Jonathan had always been stronger than his resentment of the enmity of Saul. Through his love for Jonathan, David was able to be generous. (II Samuel 9)

As for the facts of David's private life, we cannot overlook them; but we must remember that he lived about the year 1000 B.C. Among the other kings in that part of the world, he stands very high indeed. It is noteworthy that the Bible records his evil deeds quite as fully as his good ones. He was the hero of his people, but he was not "too good to be true." His sins were as much a part of him as his virtues. God used him because of the strength and nobility that were his. God could use him because he would listen.

It was quite proper for the Hebrews at that time to have many wives; the wonder is that family life among them was often very fine. No king of David's time would have thought twice before sending for the wife of any of his subjects if she pleased him, nor would he have hesitated to get rid of the husband if he objected. This is just what David did. We are told the whole story in II Samuel 11. Without any word of excuse, David had Uriah, the Hittite, placed in the front of battle so that he would be killed. Then David at once sent for Uriah's wife, Bathsheba.

It was the prophet Nathan who rebuked David, "Why have you despised the word of the LORD, to do what is evil in his sight?" Again Jehovah was requiring more of man than the heathen gods had ever asked. One of the finest points of the story is David's acceptance of this rebuke: "I have sinned against the LORD"—not only against man.

But Nathan foresaw sorrow and penance for David. He had to tell him, "The child that is born to you shall die." Later, during the illness of David and Bathsheba's little son, the king suffered and prayed and fasted, for he interpreted this illness as the result of his sin. But when the child was dead, David ceased to grieve and went to the house of the LORD to worship. His servants could not understand this. They had expected that he who had refused to eat while the child was sick would be inconsolable when he died. David said to them, "While the child was still alive, I fasted and wept; for I said, 'Who knows whether the LORD will be gracious to me, that the child may live?' But now he is dead; why should I fast? Can I bring him back again? I shall go to him, but he will not return to me."

David knew himself to be a sinner, but he also knew his God was full of mercy and kindness. He might beseech God until the moment of death; but once God had acted, David had the faith to accept God's act as righteous. (II Samuel 11–12)

The troubles of David's later days, connected with the rebellion of his son Absalom, grew out of the conditions of his court and his overindulgence of his large family. It is hard to see why Absalom should have rebelled against a father so indulgent. He was evidently a spoiled and selfish young man who inherited his father's beauty and personal charm without any of his ideas of honor and duty. For four years he secretly worked underground to steal the hearts of the men of Israel. He went around saying things like, "Oh that I were judge in the land! Then every man with a suit or cause might come to me, and I would give him justice." His revolt was so secretly carried out that when word of it came to the king's ears, David felt there was nothing for him to do but to go into exile for a time. In this he was moved largely by a desire to prevent any harm coming to the innocent citizens of Jerusalem. He also seems to have thought it possible that Absalom's treachery was a judgment of God upon him for his sins.

David would not have been in serious trouble if he had cared to take a stand. Joab's whole army was still loyal to him. The priests also were on his side. They wanted to carry the Ark out into exile with him, but David would not have that. He said, "Carry the Ark of God back into the city. If I shall find favor in the eyes of the Lord, he will bring me back . . . but if he says, 'I have no pleasure in you,' behold, here I am, let him do to me what seems good to him."

In Bashan, on the other side of Jordan, the royal forces made a stand against Absalom. It is hard to know what happened next. We are told that Bashan was thickly forested and that there was no ground suitable for battle. The Bible says more men died in the confusion of the forest than by swords and spears. Absalom had made many big mistakes. Now he made a small mistake, and it cost him his life. In the confusion of the forest paths, Absalom took a wrong turn, got separated from his followers, and came out suddenly in the midst of Joab's forces. Quickly he reigned his mule around and spurred the animal down a narrow bridle path. The overhanging branches were low, and although the mule got through, Absalom was left hanging in an oak tree. There Joab's men found him. Perhaps he was stunned by the impact of the branches, for he was unable to escape as the men stood and debated what to do. (II Samuel 15, 18)

David had forbidden anyone to hurt Absalom. While the men hesitated, Joab came up and thrust three javelins through Absalom's heart. In this deed Joab really did his master a great service, for there never could have been any peace for David or the kingdom as long as Absalom lived. But David gave himself up to passionate grief. "O my son Absalom," he cried, "my son, my son Absalom! Would I had died instead of you, O Absalom, my son, my son!"

No one could blame David for his grief, but it went beyond bounds and made him forget his duty to his people. He refused to take part in the general rejoicing until Joab again stepped in and said gruffly, "Today I perceive that if Absalom were alive and all of *us* were dead today, then you would be pleased. Now therefore arise, go out and speak kindly to your servants; for I swear by the LORD, if you do not go, not a man will stay with you this night." Those are the exact words of the Bible. Again Joab had done his master a service, but David didn't like this one any better than he liked the murder of Absalom. Back in Jerusalem David took Joab's advice and showed that he was glad to be king again, but he also took steps to put Joab in his place. (II Samuel 18–19)

David sent for Amasa, who had been Absalom's commander, and gave him Joab's command. Shortly after this replacement, a rising in the north called for military action. Amasa was told to go. Before he could get started, Joab appeared, stabbed Amasa, and took command of the men. They were so used to following Joab that they hesitated only a moment before obeying his orders as usual. Joab checked the uprising and nothing more was said about changing the command. David left it to his son, Solomon, to settle accounts with Joab. (II Samuel 20)

The events of David's early reign appeal to the imagination. But it was later on that David accomplished his most important work: the organization of the civil government and the strengthening of the national religion. Whatever personal mistakes David made, he always observed the threefold contract between king, prophet, and free people which was the ideal of Israelite monarchy. He understood responsibility as well as privilege. Although the reign of Solomon ranks high in popular estimation, David's reign was the peak of Hebrew history. David began without a square inch of land and ended with a kingdom reaching from the Mediterranean in the west to the Euphrates River in the east. When Solomon inherited this kingdom, it was well established and united. Solomon had to put up no fight for his crown. In fact, he was anointed and enthroned before his father's death. David's foresight saved Solomon from the kind of family quarrels which often follow the death of an absolute monarch who leaves several sons. (I Kings 1)

It was David who conceived the idea of building a beautiful permanent temple for the glory of Jehovah. During his lifetime, David gathered together many of the costly materials for building such a temple. (I Chronicles 22)

David was also the great poet of his people, the author of many of the psalms. Here is his last poem, expressing the way he wanted to be remembered as a poet and a king:

> Now these are the last words of David:
> The oracle of David, the son of Jesse,
>> the oracle of the man who was raised on high,
> the anointed of the God of Jacob,
>> the sweet psalmist of Israel:

> "The Spirit of the LORD speaks by me,
>> his word is upon my tongue.
> The God of Israel has spoken,
>> the Rock of Israel has said to me:
> When one rules justly over men
>> ruling in the fear of God,
> he dawns on them like the morning light,
>> like the sun shining forth upon a
>>> cloudless morning,
>> like rain that makes grass to
>>> sprout from the earth.
> Yea, does not my house stand so with God?
>> For he has made with me an everlasting covenant,
>> ordered in all things and secure.
> For will he not cause to prosper
>> all my help and my desire?"

(II Samuel 23:1–5)

## CHAPTER 16:

### KING SOLOMON

It is the tenth century before the birth of Christ. By now there have been some great names among the Hebrews, the greatest name of all being that of Moses who brought the people out of Egypt, welded them into a nation, gave them laws of worship and conduct. Following Moses in importance was David who was called by God to head a united nation and through whom all the nations of the world would be blessed.

For David this hope centered around the idea of a new place of worship, a holy temple in a holy city—Jerusalem, "a fair place, and the joy of the whole earth."

Solomon built the temple his father had envisioned. He dedicated the building to God with prayers and ceremonies David would have rejoiced to see. But Solomon also built fine palaces for himself such as David never dreamed of. He ordered an ivory throne overlaid with gold. It had six steps on which stood six lions. "There was not the like made in any kingdom." Solomon's drinking vessels were all gold; none were of silver. We are told that silver "was not considered as anything in the days of Solomon." Every three years Solomon's navy came to port, bringing gold and ivory, apes and peacocks. His court was reminiscent of the courts of the Egyptian kings in their most affluent days. Pharaoh's daughter was one of his queens. (I Kings 10:10–23)

Besides being noted for surrounding himself with luxury, Solomon had a reputation for wisdom. He is still looked upon by the Moslems as having been a master of magic with jinni and other spirits under his control, able to build palaces out of air. The First Book of the Kings says that when Solomon first came to the throne, he asked God for a special gift of wisdom that he might rule his people well. He may have really wished and prayed for that in his early days. He seems to have been quite a student of nature, knowing facts about everything that grew "from the cedar of Lebanon to the hyssop that grows out of the wall; he spoke also of beasts and of birds and of reptiles, of creeping things and of fish." Solomon also won fame from his shrewd and homely answers to popular problems which arose in courts of law. These courts were held "in the gate" of the city so that when Solomon gave a clever answer there were many to hear and marvel.

We are told of only one of Solomon's legal solutions, but it has become world-famous. Two women lived in the same house. Each woman had a baby. During the night, one of the women rolled on her baby and smothered it. In the dark, she crept over and put the dead child in the other woman's bed and took the live child into her own bed. Her friend wakened in the morning and saw the dead baby and knew it was not her own, though the other woman swore it was. The case came to Solomon. He called for a sword. "Cut the child in two," he said, "and give half to each woman." One woman remained silent. The other woman cried out, "No, let her have it. Only do not kill it." Her words, Solomon said, proved *she* was the child's real mother. (I Kings 3)

Part of Solomon's reputation for wisdom rests on his gift for coining phrases and proverbs. His name is seen in the Bible over the book of Proverbs and over Wisdom in the Apocrypha. There is fine writing and poetry in these books, but how much of them Solomon wrote we shall probably never know. The Book of Wisdom is almost certainly of a much later date.

Solomon's wisdom, then, was largely shrewdness and skill with words. He was never wise enough to see and stop his own degeneration. The trouble began in his harem —where he had seven hundred wives. First he let these women bring in idols from foreign lands. Then to please his wives he built altars for the idols. Finally, Solomon himself bowed down to idols. It was a sad end to a reign which had begun with the dedication of a magnificent temple to Jehovah! (I Kings 11)

Then, too, the splendor with which Solomon surrounded himself had to be paid for. In a small kingdom like Israel this meant heavy taxation of the people. Solomon's policy of conscripting civilians for civil service work added to the people's discontent. God sent a warning to Solomon through Jeroboam, a captain in Solomon's army. Jeroboam was told by a prophet that God would take from David's house all but the two southern tribes of Judah and Benjamin. All other tribes would be given to Jeroboam. Instead of reforming when he heard this, Solomon tried to avoid trouble by killing Jeroboam. He failed because Jeroboam took refuge in Egypt where he stayed until Solomon died.

After the death of Solomon, his young son, Rehoboam, went to Shechem, a leading northern city, evidently expecting to be crowned king. Instead he was met by a delegation led by Jeroboam. The group was respectful but had definite complaints. "Your father made our yoke heavy. Now therefore lighten the hard service of your father . . . and we will serve you." Rehoboam acted surprised although the discontent must have been well known. He asked for three days to consider and spent the time asking advice from different groups.

First Rehoboam asked the old men who had been his father's advisers. They told him it would be best to give the people fair words and promises. Then he asked the young men who had grown up with him. They told him not to yield an inch, to say to the people, "My little finger is thicker than my father's loins. And now, whereas my father laid upon you a heavy yoke, I will add to your yoke. My father chastised you with whips, but I will chastise you with scorpians."

Rehoboam took the advice of his young friends and sent arrogant words to the people of the north. For answer he got a shout of defiance. "To your tents, O Israel! Look now to your own house, David." The tax collector sent by

Rehoboam was stoned to death, and Rehoboam had to use his chariot for a quick getaway to Jerusalem. (I Kings 12)

From that time on there were two kings over the Hebrews—a king of the north, known as the king of Israel, and a king of the south, known as the king of Judah. Between the two kingdoms there was war much of the time.

PART THREE

faith and obligation

CHAPTER 17:

ELIJAH

WE ARE going to pass over three or four generations of kings, whose names are not important, in order to come to the ninth century, the age of the great prophets. During this time there had been no good kings in the north. In the year 875 we find King Ahab on the throne of Israel. ". . . Ahab did more to provoke the LORD, the God of Israel, to anger than all the kings of Israel who were before him." (I King 16:33)

Ahab was quite a leader of the neighboring kingdoms, and he was wealthy. He had a much larger kingdom than Judah, and his lands were very fertile. Also, the great trade routes between Egypt and Damascus lay across his country, and he could claim tolls from all the merchants that passed that way. Then, by his marriage, he strengthened his position even further, for he married Jezebel, daughter of the king of Sidon, a wealthy commercial city.

Now Ahab probably cared very little about religion of any kind, but his wife Jezebel cared a great deal. Coming from Sidon, she worshiped a god very closely resembling the Canaanite Baal. She must have been a very strong and determined woman, for she had her own way with her husband all through his reign, in spite of the fact that there were certainly other queens at court. Ahab had seventy sons, but Jezebel was *the* queen, no mistake about that, and she had set her mind on bringing all Israel into the service of Baal.

Remember that when the Israelites left Egypt, Moses had given them, or restored to them, the worship which was in the strongest possible contrast to the nature worship of the Near East. In the land of Canaan there was constant temptation to the Israelites because the Canaanites were always urging them to offer sacrifices to Baals. They said, "Without their help you will never get good health or fine crops." The Baals were part of the life of the land, and they were worshiped with ugly and cruel rites because they supposedly had in their power to give or withhold the rain. In a country where life itself depended upon an adequate rainfall, it is not surprising that some Hebrews were tempted to try a religious compromise. "Wouldn't it be wiser to give the Baals what they always had and make them our friends instead of our enemies?" they said.

It wasn't such a simple matter as that. The worship of Baals was a religion of wild sensual orgies with every kind of festival and procession, where all bodily restraint was cast aside, where the worshipers shouted and leaped and slashed themselves with knives. It was worse than that—

the lives of the worshipers matched their wild rites. Where
Baal was worshiped there were no Ten Commandments.
That lawlessness was what the prophets of Jehovah knew
about and fought against.

Realizing that these prophets would lead the opposition
against her, Jezebel began trying to liquidate them. This
was no easy job, for there were hundeds of prophets living
in settlements along the banks of the Jordan. They were
organized, had some sort of badge to mark them, and
held themselves ready at all times for service to the LORD.
Years later, one of Ahab's servants told Elijah that, because
he was loyal to Jehovah, he had once hidden one hundred
prophets in a cave and had secretly supplied them with
food while Jezebel searched the countryside for them.
The ninth century is sometimes called the age of the
prophets because of the fight these passionately dedicated
men put up against Baal. For a time the battle was almost
touch and go.

"Then arose Elijah the prophet and his word burned
like a torch." He came across the Jordan out of Gilead,
dressed as St. John the Baptist was to dress years later: in
a garment of hair and a girdle of leather. He went straight
as an arrow to Ahab himself. "As the LORD the God of
Israel lives, before whom I stand, there shall be neither
dew nor rain these years, except by my word." (God put
it in Elijah's mind to think and speak in His name.)

Ahab and the people ignored Elijah's warning and con-
tinued to pray to Baal. Three years of drought followed.
Elijah, of course, had to go into hiding. According to the
Bible he was fed by ravens in the desert. Later he was

cared for by a woman who was rewarded by having her son brought back to life when "there was no breath left in him." (I Kings 17)

When the word of the LORD came to Elijah again, he returned to Israel and summoned Ahab to a great contest. Ahab, desperate for lack of rain, was out hunting for patches of grass with his servants. When he saw Elijah, he cried, "Is it you, you troubler of Israel?"

Elijah answered, "I have not troubled Israel; but you have, and your father's house, because you have forsaken the commandments of the LORD and followed the Baals."

By now Ahab was ready to listen to Elijah; and according to his directions, Ahab assembled the people and four hundred and fifty prophets of Baal on the slopes of Mount Carmel. There Elijah came before them, a lone figure, and threw down his challenge. "How long will you go limping with two different opinions?" he asked. "If the LORD is God, follow him; but if Baal, then follow him."

He told them to bring two bullocks for the sacrifice—one for Baal and one for Jehovah. The prophets of Baal prepared their bullock while Elijah prepared the other. "You call on the name of your god," Elijah said, "and I will call on the name of the LORD; and the God who answers by fire, he is God." The people agreed.

Elijah offered the prophets of Baal the first chance, but he made sure there was no fire hidden under the altar, for he knew all their little tricks! The prophets must have been a little dismayed by this, but with so many eyes upon them, they didn't dare to protest, so they did as Elijah had told them. They prepared their bullock and laid it on the altar and began praying and crying aloud, "Oh Baal, hear us!"

But no voice answered. Then they worked themselves up into a frenzy and leaped on the altar, and still there was no sign.

At noon, Elijah's voice was heard in mockery. "Cry aloud," Elijah taunted. "Either he is musing, or he has gone aside, or he is on a journey, or perhaps he is asleep and must be awakened."

Louder and louder they shouted, and they began to slash themselves with knives after their custom. At last came the solemn hour of evening sacrifice in the house of the LORD. The prophets of Baal must have fallen exhausted by this time.

Elijah beckoned the people to come nearer, and then step by step he began very deliberately to make his preparation. He repaired the ruined altar of Jehovah and added twelve stones to it, one for each tribe of Israel. He put some wood in the altar and laid the divided bullock upon it. To prove that he was using no magic, he had the people pour water over the offering and in the trench all around it. Then he made his great prayer: "O LORD, God of Abraham, Isaac, and Israel, let it be known this day that thou art God in Israel, and that I am thy servant, and that I have done all these things at thy word. Answer me, O LORD, answer me, that these people may know that thou, O LORD, art God."

And fire fell and consumed the burnt offering and the wood and the stones and the dust, and licked up the water that was in the trench. And when the people saw it, they fell on their faces and cried, "The LORD, he is God! The LORD, he is God!"

Then Elijah ordered the punishment of the false

prophets. And even before Ahab could reach the palace, "the heavens grew black with clouds and wind, and there was a great rain." (I Kings 18)

The contest on Mount Carmel proved to be a turning point in the life of Elijah. Before this he seems to have been only the mouthpiece of God, rather impersonal, showing a touch of human sympathy and kindliness only when he restored life to the little child whose mother had shown him hospitality. Now here was a great triumph, but it also presented a temptation for him to take the glory to himself.

Ahab went home and told Jezebel, his wife, what had happened; but it brought no change of heart to either of them. On the contrary, Jezebel's reaction was to send a messenger posthaste to Elijah. "So may the gods do to me, and more also, if I do not make your life as the life of one of them by this time tomorrow." (She meant the false prophets whom Elijah had ordered slain.)

Should we be surprised that Elijah, who had gone though his appointed work with such courage, was dismayed at such a word from such a woman? We are told that he fled for his life. Did he have an attack of nerves? Perhaps he did, or perhaps the Almighty, with still more work for him to do, allowed him to see for a moment how little power he had in himself to help himself.

Elijah also had reason to be disheartened. The fickle people had seen a big contest and were willing enough to exalt over the defeated prophets of Baal, but how long would the impression last since the two who really mattered, Ahab and Jezebel, hadn't been impressed at all?

Elijah fled far away to the south and sat down in a desert under a juniper tree in utter discouragement. He had thought to be God's instrument in a great revival of the old faith, and nothing had come of it. It was all useless. He prayed to God that he might die. "Now, O LORD, take away my life; for I am no better than my fathers."

One thing stands out only too clearly. Up to this point, all through the great day at Carmel, Elijah had thought of nothing but God, the glory of God. Now, poor soul, he was thinking only of himself.

There he sits under the juniper tree in the south, discouraged; but God, the Father, knows just what to do with him. First, He gives Elijah what he needs desperately at this moment—sleep and food—and then He allows him to do what he wants to do. Elijah has seen his people untrue to their faith, the faith they learned long ago from Moses. His own faith is not lost, but sorely shaken. If he cannot die yet, at least he would like to go back to the place where faith was first proclaimed, to the mountain where Moses first met God face to face and had the Ten Commandments given to him.

God lets him go to Mount Horeb—but His hand is still firm on His poor servant's shoulder. Elijah comes to Horeb. All is dark and quiet there now. He climbs until he finds a little cave high up the mountainside and waits. Presently there comes a voice from heaven above, or from deep in Elijah's own heart. It really doesn't matter which. He knows perfectly well what it means—it is an accusing voice.

"What are you doing here, Elijah?"

God has let him follow his own desire, and now Elijah knows that he is not where God wants him to be. He knows, but like Adam and Eve and all the rest of us, he makes excuses, saying in effect, "I did my best for you. I did just what you told me, and no one paid any attention. They have broken down your altars and killed your prophets. I only am left, and they seek my life, too, to take it away."

The only immediate answer Elijah hears is, "Come out of that cave and stand before the LORD." He comes to the doorway of the cave, expecting some sign of the Divine Presence. But there is nothing to be seen or heard. He waits. Then the air begins to stir around him, and a great tempest sweeps up and down the mountain, and Elijah hears the rocks crashing down into the valley. But when the tempest stops, there is no presence of the LORD in the storm. And after the storm comes an earthquake, and the whole mountain shakes about him, and the presence of the LORD is not in the earthquake. And after the earthquake, the trees below his feet in the valley burst into flames, but the presence of the LORD is not in the fire. Soon afterward, Elijah hears something quite different: a soft and gentle sound that is neither voice nor silence. But Elijah knows that it is indeed the Presence. He wraps his prophet's cloak about his face and stands out in the clearing before the entrance to the cave in great awe.

Then the soft voice says again, "What are you doing here, Elijah?"

What can Elijah say? He says the same thing as before, but in a very different tone. "I did my best for you. I did just what you told me, and no one paid any attention. They have broken down your altars and killed your prophets, and I only am left and they seek my life, too, to take it away." *Now* Elijah is not making excuses. He is laying his trouble before the Lord. He is ready for any answer that may come. The answer comes in two words. "Go! Return!"

This was not just a general order. Elijah was then given three specific tasks. "Go round by the way of the wilderness and anoint Elisha, the son of Shaphat, to be prophet some day in your place," was one of the directions. God was giving Elijah a successor who would be a companion to him, too, so that he need not longer lament, "I, I only am left." (I Kings 19)

## CHAPTER 18:

### ELISHA

KING AHAB wanted a vineyard. He had plenty of vine-yards, but he got it into his head that he had to have a particular vineyard belonging to a man called Naboth. He went to Naboth and offered to buy the vineyard or exchange another vineyard for it. But Naboth said, "The LORD forbid that I should give you the inheritance of my fathers."

Ahab was not used to having his will crossed, and he behaved like a sulky child. He lay on his bed and refused to eat. Of course his wife Jezebel wanted to know what was the matter.

"Naboth will neither sell me his vineyard nor exchange it for another."

Jezebel gave Ahab a scornful look. "What kind of a king are you? My father would make short work of a man like that. Go back to your dinner and leave it to me."

What she did was to call an assembly and bribe some

witnesses to say that Naboth had cursed God and the king. This was a capital offense among the Hebrews. The law is recorded in Exodus 22:28, and, in Leviticus 24:16, punishment is designated: death by stoning. As a worshiper of Baal, Jezebel cared nothing for the Ten Commandments, but she did not hesitate to use Hebrew laws to serve her own ends. The false witnesses convinced the assembly that Naboth was guilty, and he was carried off and stoned. Ahab got his vineyard.

But Ahab's condemnation came quickly. God sent Elijah to say to him, "You have sold yourself to do what is evil in the sight of the LORD. I will bring evil upon you; I will utterly sweep you away. . . . As for Jezebel . . . the dogs shall eat Jezebel within the bound of Jezreel." (I Kings 21)

This terrible curse frightened Ahab into some expression of penitence, and the destruction of his family was put off for awhile, but his own end was not far away. In three years Ahab went to war with the Syrians. He heard that the king of Syria had assigned killers especially for him, so he went into battle in disguise. But in the words of the Bible, a Syrian "drew a bow at a venture" and the arrow struck Ahab between the joints of his armor.

When Ahab saw that he was dying, he ordered his charioteer to drive him home quickly, but he died before he got there. The chariot was full of blood, and when they took out Ahab's body, the dogs licked up the blood, as Elijah had said they would. You can read about the fate of Jezebel in II Kings 9:30–36.

Elijah lived to predict the death of Ahab's eldest son. Then it was revealed to him that his own end was near. He called his friend Elisha, and togther they started from

Gilgal at the top of the high ridge overlooking the Jordan. Descending step by step into the Jordan valley, they visited several settlements of the sons of the prophets as they passed. At each settlement, friends came out to meet and greet them. These friends whispered to Elisha, "Do you know that today the LORD will take away your master from over you?"

Elisha answered them all the same way, "Yes, I know it; hold your peace." This was no time for even pious curiosity.

It would have been natural for Elijah to want to be alone when he died, like Moses with whom he had much in common. Yet Elisha stayed with him. Somehow Elijah had to make clear to Elisha, and to those who followed, the unique duty of the prophet to forget self and live only for Jehovah.

When the two men reached the river they crossed by the same ford the Israelites had used on their way into the Promised Land. This ford was also the one by which Elijah had come in from Gilead. The crossing must have made Elijah think back over the past. Was his life work in vain? Once he had thought so. But he knew now that Jehovah controlled the destiny of His people even when things looked black.

Now Elijah asks his disciple, "Have you anything to ask of me before I go?"

Elisha answers, "Let me inherit a double share of your spirit." In Hebrew, these words refer clearly to the portion of an eldest son. They do not mean that Elisha wanted a high place among prophets. There was nothing in Elisha's long life to suggest that he was personally ambitious. This is simply his way of asking for all the strength his master can pass on to him for his future work.

But the gift Elisha wants is one only God can give, so Elijah answers, "If you see me as I am being taken from you, it shall be so." What Elijah was saying was that in every event of our lives there is a lesson God wants us to learn. Only when we have learned one day's lesson are we ready for the next. Day by day, Elisha had followed his master. Now he was to take his master's place, a harder thing to do.

If Elijah had died quietly or simply disappeared, Elisha's last day with him would still have been wonderful to remember, but Elisha was to have a vision—a scene that was full of wonder and meaning. The words of the Bible describe it: "As they still went on and talked, behold, a chariot of fire and horses of fire separated the two of them. And Elijah went up by a whirlwind into heaven. And Elisha . . . saw him no more."

Did Elisha really see a chariot and fiery horses passing between him and his master to separate them? He may have. By the gift of God, many Old Testament saints seem to have seen what it is not given all men to see. Fire is a frequent symbol of Divine Presence. Elijah had spent his life serving God. It was fitting that he should now pass into God's presence. Pictures of the flaming chariot, the horses with fiery manes and tails tossed by heavenly wind, make one truth clear: Elijah went not to death but to life. (II Kings 2:1–15)

A later incident in the life of Elisha recalls the story of Elijah's passing. There came a day when the king of Syria was very angry because Elisha had revealed his secret plans to the king of Israel. And he sent an army by night to surround the city where the prophet was. In the morning, seeing the city surrounded, the prophet's servant cried out, "Alas, my master! What shall we do?" And Elisha prayed quietly for the young man, "O LORD, I pray thee, open his eyes that he may see." The LORD opened up the servant's eyes and let him see that the mountain was full of horses and chariots of fire, and the servant knew there was nothing to fear.

The Syrian soldiers were all stricken with blindness, and Elisha led them to his own king in Samaria. But when the king asked, "Shall I smite them, my father? Shall I smite them?" Elisha answered, "Oh, no. Feed them and send them home to their own master." (II Kings 6:15–23)

The ninth century prophets were men of action. They didn't write books, but their deeds and speeches were recorded by others. Most of the information we have about them is in the form of anecdotes. This is especially true of Elisha. One of the best known stories about Elisha tells how he cured Naaman, a Syrian captain, of leprosy.

This story is told in a natural and delightful way. A little maid of Israel, a slave to Naaman's wife, said to her mistress, "Would that my lord were with the prophet who is in Samaria! He would cure him of his leprosy." Her remark found its way to the king's ears, and he sent an ambassador to Samaria demanding that the king of Israel cure Naaman.

The king was dismayed, "Syria is trying to pick a quarrel with me. How would I cure a man of leprosy?" he asked. Elisha said that he would take care of it.

Naaman came to Elisha's house with a large train of

servants, expecting to be treated with great deference. All he got was a message from within doors, "Go and wash in the Jordan seven times."

Naaman was insulted. Were not the rivers in Damascus better than the rivers in Israel? He would have gone away in a rage had not his servants persuaded him to give the remedy at least a trial. "My father, if the prophet had commanded you to do some great thing, would you not have done it?" they asked. So Naaman dipped seven times in the river Jordan, and his flesh became as the flesh of a little child. Healed, he was filled with gratitude and would have given Elisha rich rewards, but all the prophet wanted was that the people know the power of the Lord. (II Kings 5:1–16)

SUGGESTIONS FOR FURTHER READING: II Kings 4, other wonders done by Elisha in God's name.

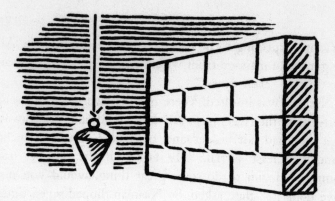

## CHAPTER 19:

### AMOS

THE mission of Elijah and Elisha was to lead the Hebrew people away from worshiping false gods. In solitude and prayer, steadfastness and self-denial, Elijah and Elisha dedicated their lives to God. But there is another kind of dedication which comes later in the lives of men and of nations. This is a searching to know what God expects of us and how we can please Him as we live together. It is a type of thinking which has to find a voice, which must speak; and because it comes out of a dedicated life and true devotion to God, it must ask questions. Sometimes it asks them of God Himself. "Why, why, must these awful things be?" From God come the answers.

To put it another way, God was seeking His people through the prophets. The prophets were impelled, often contrary to their own wishes, to speak out for God and tell the people what they needed to hear.

The men whose names are attached to the last twelve books of the Old Testament are called the "Minor Prophets" because their messages are preserved in shortened form. Amos and Hosea, however, were really very great prophets. They lived a century later than Elijah and Elisha, in the reign of Jeroboam II.

Jeroboam II, the last military king of the North, won back many lands which had been lost by the kings who had come before him. But the warfare which brought Jeroboam glory brought suffering to his subjects. Conscripted men came home to find their farms in debt, their lands mortgaged. Families unable to pay their taxes saw their property go to strangers. Because of debt, free men became slaves, dishonest merchants amassed fortunes and lived in houses furnished with silver ornaments, ivory couches, silken cushions.

The cry of the poor came to Amos, and he preached about it fearlessly. He was especially bitter against the wealthy women whom he called "cows of Bashan[1] . . . who oppress the poor, who crush the needy, who say to their husbands, 'Bring [us wine], that we may drink!'" The purpose of the Mosaic law was to prevent such oppression; but although there was now an elaborate system of worship, with big festivals kept up at the great shrines in the name of Jehovah, Amos saw that this worship was worth nothing. It led neither to right living nor to the love of God.

Amos had been a shepherd in Judah, and he came north at a time when Jeroboam was holding a victory celebration at the temple of Bethel. When the service was over and

---

[1]Bashan was noted for its fat cattle. Psalm 22.

the people were standing about in front of the temple, a shepherd in rough clothing suddenly appeared in their midst. Standing where he knew he would be heard, Amos began a terrible denunciation. His words were almost a chant. He spoke of many nations, accusing them all of the same thing: not of unfaithfulness to Jehovah—some of them never had worshiped Him—but of breaches of brotherhood and common law which should bind all men together and which all men understand. Amos is the first prophet we know of who accepted one great law for all mankind and owned that Jehovah is the God of the whole earth whether the people know it or not.

Of Damascus, the capital of Syria, Amos said, "For three transgressions of Damascus, and for four, I will not revoke the punishment; because they have threshed Gilead with threshing sledges of iron. So I will send a fire into the house of Hazael, and it shall devour the strongholds of Ben-hadad."

Then Amos thundered again: "Thus says the LORD: For three transgressions of Edom, and for four, I will not revoke the punishment; because he pursued his brother with the sword, and cast off all pity, and his anger tore perpetually, and he kept his wrath for ever. So I will send a fire upon Teman, and it shall devour the strongholds of Bozrah."

Every one of the neighboring nations, in turn, was accused and its punishment foretold. Think how the Israelites must have cheered as they heard the doom upon the nations they hated! Then Amos came to Judah, and he said this: "For three transgressions of Judah, and for four,

I will not revoke the punishment; because they have rejected the law of the Lord, and have not kept his statutes, but their lies have led them astray, after which their fathers have walked. So I will send a fire upon Judah, and it shall devour the strongholds of Jerusalem."

Now, at last, with the rhythmic tide of his speech sweeping his listeners along, Amos spoke of Israel: "For three transgressions of Israel, and for four, I will not revoke the punishment; because they sell the righteous for silver, and the needy for a pair of shoes—they that trample the head of the poor into the dust of the earth, and turn aside the way of the afflicted . . . they lay themselves down beside every altar upon garments taken in pledge; and in the house of their God they drink the wine of those who have been fined."

Then he continued as if God were speaking: "I brought you up out of the land of Egypt, and led you forty years in the wilderness, to possess the land of the Amorite." Amos listed God's kindnesses; then he announced: "Hear this word that the Lord hath spoken against you, O people of Israel, against the whole family which I brought up out of the land of Egypt: 'You only have I known of all the families of the earth; therefore I will punish you for all your iniquities.' " That was the great sin of the Israelites, as Amos saw it: God had done more for them than for any nation in the world. He had made them His own people. He could expect much of them. Therefore their sin would be held against them.

Five times Amos warned the Israelites and begged them to reform, to return to the Lord "Seek good, and not evil," he cried, "that you may live; and so the LORD, the God of hosts, will be with you." (There was still that promise of mercy!)

In the name of God Amos spoke out against hypocrisy, too. "I hate, I despise your feasts, and I take no delight in your solemn assemblies. Even though you offer me your burnt offerings and cereal offerings, I will not accept them, and the peace offerings of your fatted beasts I will not look upon. Take away from me the noise of your songs; to the melody of your harps I will not listen. But let justice roll down like waters, and righteousness like an everflowing stream."

Amos once described God as setting a plumb line in the midst of his people. Just as surveyors test a wall to see if it is upright and true, so God is judging His people, he said. Amos has been called the prophet of righteousness, and righteousness includes justice. (Amos 7:8)

Remember Abraham, whose faith was counted to him for righteousness? At the time when he prayed for the sinners in Sodom, he said to his nephew Lot, "Shall not the judge of all the earth do right?" Of course there cannot really be justice without love. It is only a limitation in our minds that sometimes sees conflict between justice and love. Perhaps the writings of the two prophets, Amos and Hosea, are given to us to show us that in the Divine Love there is no conflict; both love and justice are finally realized in ways that God understands better than we. (Amos 1–5)

## CHAPTER 20:

### HOSEA

HOSEA is the prophet of love. He deplores the same social sins as Amos. "There is no faithfulness or kindness, and no knowledge of God in the land; there is swearing, lying, killing, stealing, and committing adultery; they break all bounds and murder follows murder." To Hosea all this grows out of Israel's unfaithfulness to God—her forgetfulness of all His benefits during her long history. This ingratitude is the source sin, the sin which lies at the back of all others. It is the worst sin of all, because it is a sin against love. (Hosea 4:1-2)

This belief Hosea shares with all the later prophets. Isaiah, Jeremiah, Ezekiel, are all prophets of love, but Hosea's own particular task is to try to make people understand their true relationship to God, that it is a relationship of love.

In his youth, like other great prophets, Hosea had given

himself to the service of God. Thinking over the history of his people and all that God had done for them, he was filled with passionate grief for their degeneration. Hosea was able, as few would have been, to see ingratitude in terms of the divine disappointment, the disappointment of the Heavenly Love. With that in mind, he was called to a severe task which few men would have accepted even from the hand of God. Hosea's life was to be an active parable, and it was through his account of his life that he was able to show, not only to his own people but to us also, the picture of Divine Love, that Love that will not let us go, however unfaithful we may be. (Hosea 1—3)

Hosea's task was to love one who rejected his love. We know that the New Testament makes this the perfection of Christian charity: to be patient with the unlovable, to care for them without shrinking. We have seen that done by Christian people in many different relationships since the Christian era began. But this, you see, is the eighth century *before* Christ, when nothing was yet known of the love of our Lord Jesus for sinners and outcasts. How unlovable these people were! Hosea never could have done what he did without the help of what we now call Grace. This is his story.

The young Hosea had seen a woman named Gomer who at sight seemed lovable. At the same time he could see in her a restlessness, a fickleness, which didn't promise a happy marriage. Now it would have been perfectly natural for him to put her out of his thoughts and look for somebody else. But in the midst of these thoughts came the word from the Almighty, to whom his life was dedicated, and the Almighty told Hosea to make Gomer his wife, even though she might be unfaithful.

So Hosea took Gomer to his home, and she stayed with him for a while. Then one day she left him. Perhaps she passed by one of those temples of Baal where they hired women to take part in the wild singing and dancing that were part of the services of such temples. How dull in comparison was Hosea's quiet home! He might try to coax Gomer back, but she didn't take long to choose: Hosea could take care of the children if he liked; she was off!

It is hard to trace the order of events after this, but the second chapter of the Book of Hosea suggests that the prophet made more than one effort to win back his erring wife by loving appeals. First he sent the children to plead with her, but that was a failure. In the following verse it is impossible to distinguish his own experience from that of the God he serves, who has given Hosea the wonderful and terrible experience of sharing in some measure the agony of his Creator. The whole chapter is in the language of love. "I will . . . bring her into the wilderness, and speak tenderly to her."

Was this again a failure? It seems that it was. Hosea says, "So I bought her." She may have become a slave either of the temple or of some other man from whom Hosea bought her back. And now the command of God was *love*. God didn't say just "take" her, "put up with" her. The word was *love*.

Now how could he? Love, as we ordinarily understand the word, can't be had to order. What was it that made it possible for Hosea? Just one thing. He already loved God, and he believed that what God told him to do, he would have the power to perform. Winning Gomer was a harder task than before. She was not likely to be pleased, because she would have to stay at home. According to the law, she was now her husband's property. It was not likely to be at all a happy home. We don't really know how it came out. There are suggestions of a reconciliation at last.

We can't be sure, because at this point in the story Hosea drops his personal account and the writing melts away into the story of the eternal love between God and His people; God revealed to Hosea what his experience meant. It was the true story of God's own unending love for Israel. He wanted to show the world, through Hosea, how deep and how unearned that love could be.

Yet the people of the northern kingdom had refused God's love for so long that when the message of Hosea came to them, it was too late. In a few years the Assyrians conquered the northern kingdom and deported most of the population. The people were swallowed up in the midst of the Assyrian empire. The northerners became the "ten lost tribes" and disappeared forever from secular and sacred history.

Fortunately, someone escaped to Jerusalem in the kingdom of Judah, carrying with him the words and message of Hosea. The message of God's love was read and studied by the prophet Isaiah and his successors.

## CHAPTER 21:

### ISAIAH

THE kingdom of Judah, to which Isaiah belonged, lasted one hundred and fifty years longer than Israel, probably because Judah's kings made some serious efforts to bring about reforms. There is a brief account of these years in the Second Book of Kings, but a more lifelike story comes to us from the prophets.

The prophet Isaiah rose to prominence just before the captivity of Israel. Like Amos and Hosea, Isaiah raised his voice against hypocrites, cruel women in fine clothes, landgrabbers who "grind the faces of the poor and lay field to field" (that is, buy up the poor people's lands).

Isaiah knew better than any prophet who had gone before that religion and conduct have to be brought together—one depends upon the other, and they cannot be separated. The only hope for Judah lay in the revival of her religion.

Isaiah, like Amos, realized that all nations are bound together, and that God is the God of all the earth. He also had one of those grand visions of the glory of the LORD which God gives only to those who have power to see what other men cannot. Isaiah was a member of the priesthood, but he was not holding any special office. The story of his vision belongs to a day when he was merely worshiping with the people in the Temple.

If you have even a general idea of what those morning and evening services in the Temple were like, you will see how Isaiah's vision grew out of his surroundings. He was standing among the other worshipers in a great, high-walled court open to the sky. In the morning the service was one of sacrifice at the great, twenty-four-foot-square altar. Every morning at least one lamb, and sometimes many animals, were offered in the name of the people. The sacrifice was meant as a sign that the covenant between God and His people never should cease; the fire on this altar was never allowed to go out, day or night. If you climbed to one of the hills around the city and looked down, you would always see the little pall of smoke hanging over the altar.

In front of the worshipers in the court was the actual Temple building, sixty or seventy feet high, with twelve steps leading up to it. The whole front of that building was usually closed by high, folding doors, but twice a day the priests went in. They climbed the steps and slipped the doors back for a few moments. (You may recall the story of Zechariah before the birth of John the Baptist, when he had to go up those steps and into the temple on some sort of duty.)

When the priest rolled back the doors, the people watching down in the court saw, just for a moment, the inside of the Temple. In the center of the building, and before the door to the Holy Place, was a golden altar on which the incense was replenished every morning. On one side of that altar stood a golden table where lay the holy bread only the priests could eat, and on the other side stood a seven-branched lamp stand. As the priests went in and out, the gentle wind of their entry would make the lamps flare for a moment. Then the people would see a little more than otherwise.

Behind the priest, as he entered, they could see the altar and the table and the lamp stand. They could see that there was something else behind them; there was another little room which was always closed except once a year. This room was shut off from the Holy Place by a wonderful curtain, very beautifully embroidered in bright colors—blue and purple and scarlet. In that flash of a moment when the door was opened, the people could see that the forms embroidered on the curtain were great winged figures, like winged lions, called cherubim, and with them were palm trees and opened flowers. So Isaiah tells us. Of course he had seen the curtains many times at the opening of the door.

He tells us that he had been meditating on sad and terrible things. One was the memory of a king who had done well in his day, but had just died in dishonor. Isaiah had been thinking of all the failures of his people and his own utter helplessness to put anything right. This day, when the door was opened, it seemed to Isaiah that he saw all that was inside in a glow of light with incense

smoke rising. Then it seemed to him that the great cherubim embroidered on the curtain detached themselves from
the curtain and flew upward into the sky above the roof
of the Temple. They flew up until there was a host of them
in the air above, and they were singing all together,
thronging above a vast throne, the throne of God. Isaiah
couldn't see anyone on the throne, but it seemed as if a
glory streamed every way on either side and filled the
whole Temple court. What the cherubim and seraphim
were singing was a song that we know well, "Holy, holy,
holy, is the LORD of Hosts; the whole earth is full of
his glory!" Isaiah was filled with fear and dread because
he felt that he was unworthy to see such a sight and hear
such a song; and he cried out, "Woe is me! For . . . I am
a man of unclean lips, and I dwell in the midst of a people
of unclean lips; for my eyes have seen the King, the LORD
of Hosts!"

Then, out of the throngs above the Temple, one seraph
flew down to the great altar of sacrifice in the court, and
with a pair of tongs he took from the altar one glowing
coal, and he laid it on Isaiah's lips and said to him, "Behold,
this has touched your lips; your guilt is taken away, and
your sin forgiven."

Isaiah continues, "I heard the voice of the Lord saying,
'Whom shall I send, and who will go for us?' Then I said,
'Here am I! Send me.'" That was Isaiah's call. That was
the moment of his call. And the meaning of his call? To
stand there in the presence of God and to receive messages
for Him, and to carry the messages to those to whom
God should send him. (Isaiah 6)

It is interesting to realize that the idea of God speaking

in this way to his prophets was not so strange at that time
as it might seem to us. We can't picture what life must
have been to those men who were called to stand alone
in the world like that and utter messages terrible to hear,
but which yet must be spoken. Often, so very often, they
knew the people would not heed the messages or care for
them at all. That knowledge added to the spiritual suffering
the prophets went through. It was almost as if God had to
give them some special consolation, some special thing to
make life more bearable. And this idea, as you can see, was
not an unusual one for those who have studied the ways
of God.

We have been led by many great thinkers to believe that
everything that happens means far more than what we see
and what we think. The prophets saw a lot of things that
were plain and clear happening around them; and then, soon
after, it was just as if they saw *through* them to what we
cannot see, but what God wanted them to see.

Now something like this happened to Isaiah around the
year 725. In that year Isaiah's king—his name was Ahaz—
heard a rumor. In fact, Ahaz saw plain signs that the king
of Israel and the king of Syria, his two worst enemies,
were coming down into Judah and were going to fight
against him there. The hearts of the king and his people
were shaken with terror, like trees shaking in the wind.
At that point, God gave Isaiah a message, and the message
was that Ahaz should be calm and quiet. In a very little
time, God said, the two kings would be destroyed by a
much greater king, the king of Assyria. If Ahaz didn't
believe this, he would have no comfort or help. And
then the voice of God, through Isaiah, told Ahaz to ask

for a sign that this would be. But Ahaz wouldn't believe, and he wouldn't ask for any sign. As a matter of fact, he had a plan of his own to defend his country, so he said, "I will not ask." (Isaiah 7:1–17)

Isaiah insisted that God would give Ahaz a sign anyway, because time was short. He told Ahaz of a young woman in his court who would soon be married and bear a son whose name would be Immanuel, meaning "God is with us." Before this baby should learn the difference between right and wrong, the kings Ahaz feared would be carried away by the king of Assyria.

But Ahaz didn't feel like trusting God or sitting quietly. He went right off to the king of Assyria on his own and asked for help, offering to pay him a large tribute if he would go and destroy the kings of Syria and Judah.

Now that was very hard on Isaiah, who had spoken from his heart. He would have been in despair if it hadn't been that at that moment God put into the heart of Isaiah a wonderful thought: that none of God's promises, from Abraham, all along the line, up to these promises now being spoken—none of them would ever fail! None of God's promises ever do. Like Ahaz, Isaiah had only to be quiet and wait and trust in the LORD.

Then came a series of beautiful thoughts and hopes which hung on the promise that there should be a child unlike any other child, God's own child . . . "and the government will be upon his shoulder, and his name will be called Wonderful Counselor, Mighty God, Everlasting Father, Prince of Peace. Of the increase of his government and of peace there will be no end, upon the throne of

David, and over his kingdom, to establish it, and to uphold it with justice and with righteousness from this time forth and for evermore. The zeal of the LORD of hosts will do this." Isaiah heard these words, but he was not privileged to know where and when they were to come true. (Isaiah 9:6–7)

Three of the men who wrote the New Testament Gospels were Hebrews, and the fourth, St. Luke, may have been. All four knew their Old Testament, so it was perfectly natural for St. Matthew, who wrote the first Gospel, to relate what happened in Galilee to the promise heard by Isaiah. Matthew quotes these beautiful verses which all Christendom has felt, in the fullest sense, to be really prophetic of the far future—first the Child of David's line, then a promise of light in the stricken land of Galilee. Our Lord walked in Galilee. He was to be the Great Light in Galilee which had been so dark. (Isaiah 9:2 and St. Matthew 4:16)

That was one of Isaiah's greatest visions. There are other visions we cannot go into, but there is an event in Isaiah's life we should think about.

When Ahaz died, his son Hezekiah turned to Isaiah for advice. Isaiah told Hezekiah that he must bring back true religion, with obedience to the laws of Jehovah taking precedence over showy sacrifices. Hezekiah ordered the Passover to be remembered, and he had the holy places redecorated and cared for. But military threats interrupted his reforms.

Judah lay between Egypt and Mesopotamia. Sennacherib, king of Assyria, wanted Egypt. Judah lay in his path.

Sennacherib was so anxious to get to Egypt that he by-passed Jerusalem and went along the coast through the Philistine cities. The Philistines put up a fight, and succeeded in delaying the Assyrians on the border of Egypt.

While Sennacherib was encamped on the Egyptian border, he sent a message to Hezekiah saying, in effect, "I am coming to get your city on my way back. In the meanwhile, tell your people to sit quietly and I will take them where they will be much better off than they are here."

Hezekiah sent for Isaiah, who gave him the same advice he had given Ahaz. Isaiah said that, since Hezekiah's tiny army was hopelessly outclassed, it would be best for the Judahites to keep calm and cross their bridges when they came to them. (Isaiah 36 and 37; also II Chronicles 32)

As it turned out, there were no bridges to cross. The Bible says that an angel passed through the host of Sennacherib, killing so many of his men that he had to give up the Egyptian campaign. One explanation is that an epidemic swept through the Assyrian camp. Isaiah mentions also that Sennacherib got word that his throne at home was in danger. Whatever his personal reasons were, Sennacherib returned to Assyria because God intended him to do so. On a cylinder which is now in the British Museum, Sennacherib's account of his campaign claims the capture of many cities, but not of Jerusalem. "Hezekiah I shut up like a bird in a cage," Sennacherib boasts. He does not add that shortly after he arrived home his own empire was seized by the Babylonians.

Hardly anybody reads Sennacherib's cylinder. But the

Book of Isaiah is one of the most quoted parts of the Bible, not only because of its important message but also because of the beauty of its wording.

> The wolf shall dwell with the lamb,
>   and the leopard shall lie down with the kid,
> and the calf and the lion and the fatling together,
>   and a little child shall lead them.

(Isaiah 11:6)

## CHAPTER 22:

## THE EXILE

THE stories of the heroes of Israel have constantly brought us back to the idea of sacred history. Sacred history always means one thing—the intention of God to bring back the world to Himself that it may "become the kingdom of God and His Christ." This purpose is being worked out by a wonderful process which no man can see or fully understand.

But although we cannot see the process, we can look back and see through all the great events of ordinary history a definite pattern taking shape. Sometimes we can even see something of the steps by which mankind has reached the point where we now stand. Of course we shall never fully understand, but if we fill our minds with the thought of the greatness and glory of God, His plan will come clearer. That is exactly where the Bible can help us, if we allow it to. We shall find our hearts uplifted and our will to serve God strengthened, as we say in the words of one of the psalms: "The LORD hath done great things to us already; wherefore we rejoice." That is the song the Jews themselves used to sing on their pilgrimages to the Holy City, in spite of all the sorrow and losses they had suffered.

In man, as part of his nature, is the desire to serve God. In man, also, is the desire to serve himself, to further what he considers his own best interests. The result of these two desires living together in one heart is conflict. Man does not really know what his own best interests are. That is why we pray at Easter: "Almighty God, who through thine only-begotten Son Jesus Christ hast overcome death, and opened unto us the gate of everlasting life; We humbly beseech thee that, as by thy special grace preventing [leading] us thou dost put into our minds good desires, so by thy continual help we may bring the same to good effect . . ."[1]

That sums up the whole of the Christian life. God is putting good desires into men's minds always, everywhere, and helping us bring them to good effect. But God does not move His creatures like puppets on strings. He gives them the power to choose good or evil, but not without showing them through the pattern of history where each choice leads. A study of history, secular and sacred, makes the greatness and glory of God come clearer. Events arrange themselves into a definite pattern. The forces of darkness never fully succeed, but God's purposes are advanced through all generations.

God did great things for Israel. He gave the people a

---

[1] Collect, page 163, *Book of Common Prayer.*

promise, a hope, and a goal, and at each stage He gave them a demonstration of His love and mercy. Usually this demonstration took the form of a great deliverance. But not always.

In our imaginations, we can watch a long straggling line of men and women trudge wearily across the desert toward Babylon. Judah is no more, and its citizens are making a forced trek into captivity. It is the kind of death march that made headlines during World War II. How can this be part of God's plan? Ahead of the people of Judah lies a country of unknown laws and idol worship. Behind lies a system of worship and a law of life often disregarded but better, nevertheless, than the worship of any other nation. That it is better, is one of the things the exiles need to learn.

In Babylon, the Hebrews came to value their religion as they had never done in Judah. It suddenly became imperative to appoint scribes to go over the old records and set them in order, and to write what was believed to be true. This work was one of the most important outcomes of the Babylonian exile. It was possible because the Jews were not ill treated in Babylon. In fact, the Babylonians considered it wise policy to keep the Jews contented so that there would be less chance of rebellion and so that the captives would do more work. The Jews were skillful and intelligent, and many of them worked their way into fine positions in Babylon. Some of these prosperous exiles stopped yearning for home and the old faith. But, as in the past, a few men and women were able to keep the light of faith and hope burning, and it was still the work of the prophets to hold fast the faith.

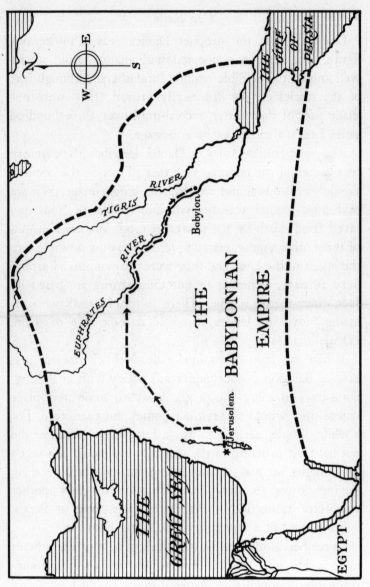

THE EXILE

One of these, the prophet Daniel, was a mysterious figure. His name is connected with many heroic stories well known to our Bible-reading forefathers. Although few of the stories can be historically proved (they were not made part of the written record until over three hundred years later), they do carry a message.

The most familiar story of Daniel describes his resistance to a decree of the reigning king that all men in the country should kneel down and worship the king's image. We are told how Daniel was thrown into a den of lions and saved from death by the power of God. We are also told of three other young men who refused to bow down before the image of the king, and they were thrown into a burning fiery furnace. Whether or not these stories are based on fact, their theme is true. There *were* Hebrews who remained loyal to Jehovah, and God took care of them. (Daniel 6: 10–28)

When the Jews went into exile, Nebuchadnezzar was king of Babylon. Nebuchadnezzar's policy with small kingdoms was to carry the people away to some new place where they would forget their homes and patriotism. For a while the plan seemed to work. But Nebuchadnezzar did not have the ordering of the world in his hands. Just when he thought he was accomplishing his purpose, he died, leaving no son to carry on. Within a few years another conqueror came out of the east. Cyrus, king of Persia, became ruler of a vast empire including Babylon.

Cyrus had a different way of dealing with small, difficult nations. His way was to let them go back to their homelands. He reasoned that liberated exiles would be grateful enough to serve him fairly willingly. So in the year 538,

Cyrus issued a decree saying that the Jews and other exiles in Babylon could go home. This is a place where we can see secular history being shaped to God's purpose.

The Bible points out that Cyrus was fulfilling a prophecy made by Jeremiah: "Now in the first year of Cyrus king of Persia, that the word of the LORD by the mouth of Jeremiah might be accomplished, the LORD stirred up the spirit of Cyrus king of Persia so that he made a proclamation throughout all his kingdom and also put it in writing: 'Thus says Cyrus king of Persia, "The LORD, the God of heaven, has given me all the kingdoms of the earth, and he has charged me to build him a house at Jerusalem, which is in Judah. Whoever is among you of all his people, may the LORD his God be with him. Let him go up." ' " (II Chronicles 36:22–23)

## CHAPTER 23:

### THE NEW ISRAEL

THE exile lasted more than fifty years. Some Jews built houses in Babylon, went into business, prospered, and thought little about the past. Others still hoped for return, remembering the old religion and dreaming of a higher and better way of keeping the law.

When Cyrus made his liberating proclamation, some exiles received the news with joy and wanted to leave at once. But the exhortations in Chapters 40—50 of Isaiah show us what efforts had to be made to arouse the people as a whole to action. There were more who were willing to contribute to the expenses than to go home themselves.

The story of the return is told in the book of Ezra. From cylinders written by Cyrus himself, and now in the British Museum, we learn that the first band set out in the year 535. It was led by Zerubbabel, a prince of the house of David. Zerubbabel had been appointed governor but was never given the title of king. Jeshua, the high priest, seems to have had equal rank. Once God had given the people Joshua, whose name meant "God is salvation." Now he was giving them Jeshua, whose name also means "God saving." One day God would send Jesus to *be* God saving.

When the exiles reached Jerusalem, even before they built homes, they set up a new altar on the stone base which had survived the destruction of the city. On this altar, Zerubbabel and Jeshua offered morning and evening sacrifices from that day forth. (Ezra 3)

Their next thought was to rebuild the Temple. Foundations were laid at a happy service of dedication with "songs of trumpets and songs of harps." Praise and thanks were given to God in song: "For his mercy endureth forever." Young men shouted for joy; old men, a few of whom had seen the Temple destroyed, wept aloud.

The work had many interruptions. While the exiles were in Babylon, people of mixed origins had moved into Judah. Most of these people professed the Jewish religion and wanted to help build the Temple. They were settled, had more resources than the returned exiles had, and they seemed at least outwardly reverent, but the Hebrews were so anxious to turn back the clock and make everything exactly as it had been that they were afraid to accept help.

As a result, the landholders, later called Samaritans, became enemies instead of friends. They planned many an intrigue at the Persian court in an effort to halt the temple-building program. But despite poverty and opposition, the Temple was rebuilt and Hebrew resettlement continued.

Because there was much correspondence between Jerusalem and the Persian court, Nehemiah, a devout Hebrew cupbearer to the king of Persia, learned that the walls of Jerusalem were still in ruins. Nehemiah tells how he took advantage of his nearness to the king to put in a plea for permission to rebuild Jerusalem's walls. It was dangerous to take a personal matter to the king, even when the king was in a good mood. But Nehemiah's actions were motivated by prayer, and he got not only the king's permission to go, but also a troop of soldiers to protect him from any opposition the landowners might put up.

This was about 445 years before Christ, approximately one hundred years after the first return. The walls of Jerusalem were rebuilt at Nehemiah's direction. He divided the work among all inhabitants. Even the priests helped. And everyone who wielded a shovel or pickax or trowel, also carried a sword. It was an enterprise which could not have been completed without the inspiring leadership of a prayerful man like Nehemiah. (Nehemiah 1–5)

It is at about this period in history that the main work of reviving the Jewish religion was completed. The daily routine of sacrifice and service in the Temple was reestablished and maintained. Also Ezra is credited with getting the sacred books in order.

In the year 331, Alexander the Great flashed like a meteor across the Near East. Before he died, in 323, he had made himself master of Egypt and of all the Persian Empire, and had spread his rule over all Asia Minor as far as India. Before long most Jews outside Palestine knew no language but Greek. Around 200 B.C. the Old Testament was translated into Greek. God was clearing paths for spreading the Christian story which was soon to come.

Another momentous happening occurred about this same

time. The king of Syria, under whose rule the Palestine Jews had just come, was a man of great ambition. His name was Antiochus IV. Antiochus decided that all countries under his rule should have one religion and culture: his own. It was not hard for him to make Asia Minor comply. It was not even hard for him to get into Jerusalem and take the steps he thought would accomplish his purpose. Among other desecrations, Antiochus ordered the image of the Olympian god Zeus to be set up on the high altar in the Temple at Jerusalem. The Second Book of the Maccabees in the Apocrypha tells the torture and persecution to which Antiochus subjected the Jews. But he went too far and found himself with a revolt on his hands.

The Maccabean revolt, led by Judas Maccabeus, was successful. Afterward the Jews had an independent kingdom of their own which continued until the year 69 B.C. Unfortunately, the family which succeeded the Maccabees had no right to high priesthood, but made themselves priests anyway. They lied and cheated and fought among themselves for office. Finally, in the year 69, their intrigues and rivalries led them to ask the Roman general Pompey to arbitrate for them. Pompey obliged by putting the whole nation under the jurisdiction of the Roman Empire.

A long period of probation had come to an end. There were, of course, still many devout Jews. Their lives influenced many Gentiles to turn to the one true God. These converted Gentiles were called proselytes and were allowed to share in some of the rites of the Jews. We read of proselytes in the Book of Acts, and learn that when the Gospel was preached, many of them became Christians.

During the last century before our Lord's coming, the

faithful turned eagerly to sacred writing to keep their hope alive. The psalms describe the kind of king they had all looked for at one time. Now, too many Jews were looking for a military leader. They made that only too clear when Jesus was born. St. John says, "He came to his own home, and his own people received him not." There were a few exceptions, and St. Luke speaks about these few—looking for redemption in Jerusalem, faithful all the days of their lives. These were the people who were friends of Simeon and Anna, and the friends of our Lord. These were the people who welcomed our Lord's coming even in poverty and in obscurity, and some are said to have recognized Him immediately in that lowly guise in which He came. (St. John 1:11 and St. Luke 2:25–38)

But the ruling powers of Judea said of our Lord, "We will not have this man to reign over us." And the people took up the cry. On Calvary, Israel threw away the wonderful promise the Hebrews had long cherished. There, except for our Lord Himself, the old covenant ended.

Still God loved. He gave the world a new promise. At the Last Supper Jesus said, "This is the new covenant in my blood." The only way to enter the new covenant is by personal acceptance of Jesus Christ. After the resurrection, even the disciples had to re-enter the covenant. From that time on, baptism (signifying acceptance of Jesus as the Messiah) has been required of all who would be Christians.

We find the voice of the Church speaking in the records of St. Luke: There is only one way; "repent, and be baptized every one of you in the name of Jesus Christ." Thus and only thus could the old Jews become members of the new covenant. So Paul and Peter and John held out this invitation not only to the Jews, but to all who would become God's new chosen people, the new Israel, the Christian Church. (Acts 2:38)

What of the old Israel? It survives as a gifted people with whose long-drawn-out sorrows we must all have sympathy. St. Paul was grieved because his own race, a wonderful race with a wonderful past, was no longer to be called God's chosen people. By their own choice, they had cut themselves off from the promise of salvation. And only by their own choice (as individuals or as a nation), can they become part of God's new chosen people.

The word *salvation* is used over and over in the Bible. Zechariah, father of St. John the Baptist, speaks of salvation several times. He is not talking about going to heaven when you die. He is talking about being redeemed, made whole in spirit, here and now. Having shown his faith by obediently naming his son John (although no one in his family had ever borne the name), Zechariah was "filled with the Holy Spirit," and prophesied, saying,

> Blessed be the Lord God of Israel,
> for he has visited and redeemed his people,
> and has raised up a horn of salvation for us
> in the house of his servant David . . .
> (St. Luke 1:68–79)

This glorious hymn of praise has become part of our service of Morning Prayer, the Benedictus, on page 14 of the Prayer Book. All that it says of the Old Testament hopes, we realize with Zechariah in the Person of our Lord.

Simeon, a man who had spent his long life in prayer and

worship, also recognized Christ as "salvation." When the infant Jesus was brought to the Temple, Simeon took Him up in his arms and blessed God and said,

> Lord, now lettest thou thy servant
>     depart in peace,
>      according to thy word;
>   for mine eyes have seen thy salvation
> which thou hast prepared in the
>     presence of all peoples,
> a light for revelation to the Gentiles,
> and for glory to thy people Israel.
>            (St. Luke 2:29–32)

These words, which we call the Nunc dimittis, are also found in our Prayer Book, page 28.

Salvation is something which has been going on since the first rainbow spread across the sky after the flood. It is not finished yet. It is the most important work in the world, and God lets us help Him do it. A Christian, from the day of his baptism forward, has this glorious purpose for living.

## CHAPTER 24:

### GROWING IN FAITH

THOSE who were in close association with Jesus while He was on earth were increasingly aware of His power. When they failed to heal the sick as He did, He told them that it was because of the weakness of their faith: ". . . For truly, I say to you, if you have faith as a grain of mustard seed, you will say to this mountain, 'Move hence to yonder place,' and it will move; and nothing will be impossible to you." A mustard seed is so small you can scarcely see one in the palm of your hand, but an amount of faith as small as that brings strength to those who have it. So the apostles begged of Jesus, "Increase *our* faith!" (St. Matthew 17:20 and St. Luke 17:5)

And we may well ask, "Where does faith begin with us? With me?" Where does it start, and how does it grow? These are questions we ought to think about more often.

In each one of you there is a spirit which is the direct gift of God. This spirit is made in the image and likeness of God and can grow in the knowledge of God. It is the center of your personality, of yourself, of *you*. Our schools try to give you healthy bodies and intelligent minds, but they do not say much to you about your spirit. They do not often tell you that your spirit is intended to control both body and mind, and that it can only do this if it has found for itself a meeting place where it can know God as those Old Testament heroes did, as a friend. This meeting with God is not a matter of learning. You will find it described in the twenty-seventh Psalm: "Thou hast said, 'Seek ye my face.' My heart says to thee, 'Thy face, LORD, do I seek.' "

"Thy face, LORD, do I seek" brings us, of course, to the place of prayer. The foundation of prayer is in the knowledge and love of God. But how do we get the knowledge and love of God? It used to be learned largely from the Bible; and it still can be, if we know how to look for it. At the very beginning of the Bible we find an example of the most natural and easiest kind of prayer.

The first chapters of the Bible describe men and women at their daily work, knowing quite well that God is somewhere in the garden, that they may meet Him at any time. Especially in the evening, in the cool of the day when work is laid aside, there was leisure for pleasant conversation with friends and, above all, with God. It was something these people looked forward to—before they sinned. It was only *after* they sinned that they did not feel at home with God any more. Something had come between.

Now of course that sense of happiness in the presence of God wasn't lost forever. Those who sinned learned to be sorry and begin over again. Remember, it was never God who hid His face from them. It was they who hid their faces from God. As we read on in the Bible, we find how God was always opening new ways for men to come back to Him. Happily, there were always some who wanted to come back. When they did, they were able to talk to God again.

In those early chapters of the Bible, we often come upon a phrase which seems strange to us, but to the Hebrews it seemed just right. We hear of men *walking* with God. In the list of the patriarchs before the Flood we read, "Enoch walked with God." That's all we know about him, except that "He *was* not, for God took him." (The Jews think this means that he was taken to heaven without dying.) Then we read later that "Noah walked with God" in the midst of people who cared nothing for God and laughed at Noah for building the ark. (Note that Noah was Enoch's great-grandson; some kind of good tradition had evidently been kept up.) Again we find God saying of Abraham, "Walk before me and be thou perfect." This word *walk* occurs often later in the Bible and especially in the Psalms. "Blessed are those whose way is blameless, who *walk* in the law of the LORD!" Plainly it means much the same as the word *live*. They "lived their lives" with God— not as if they were always in church, but more like Adam and Eve in the garden, as if God was always there where *they* were, as if He was never a stranger. And what is this but a kind of prayer? Do you remember that St. Paul once said, "Pray constantly"? No doubt you wanted to answer, "Perfectly impossible!" Well, St. Paul must have meant something like "walk with God at all times." (I Thessalonians 5:17)

We don't expect to be as much at home with Almighty God as Abraham and Moses were. But we read in the Bible of many people who did talk with Him quite naturally. They were not always asking Him for things, either. Sometimes, like Job or Jonah or Jeremiah, they argued with Him. So did St. Paul in New Testament times!

All these people had to have special places and times when they worshiped God together and joined one another in praising Him for what He is and what He does. That is what we call corporate prayer. Usually we learn prayer best by praying together. That is why we take very small children to church before they can understand much about the service. At first they have only a dim idea that this is a place where God is. But as soon as they can understand ever so little, we try to teach them to speak to God, each for himself. Then the two ways fit together. They turn into the "walking and talking" that we hear of so often in the Bible. Only by such "walking and talking" can we reach the "knowledge of God which is the foundation of all prayer." That, you know, was our Lord's last prayer for His disciples. He said to God, "This is eternal life, that they know thee the only true God, and Jesus Christ whom thou hast sent." (St. John 17:3)

The author of the Letter to the Hebrews gave us some wonderful words about Moses when he wrote of him, "He endured as seeing him who is invisible." He *endured:* he put up with all that wandering in the desert; with all those provoking, contradictious people; and he died at last on the far side of the river, outside the Promised Land. "He endured," because he was perfectly sure that the way was always open between himself and God, perfectly sure that God was always right. This ideal of faith which the author of our Letter to the Hebrews constantly puts before us is, when you think of it, a double pledge. God begins it (as with Abraham), and we reply with trust. He gives the task and the challenge. We answer with a pledge of loyalty.

This is the foundation of our faith. How can we keep it alive?

One way is through prayer. Perhaps the best kind of prayer is a kind which is open to all men, women, and children alike, the instinctive way even of the very ignorant. This is a special kind of prayer which has a very long name but takes only a very short time. It is called "ejaculatory" prayer. From your grammar you know what an ejaculation is; the term comes from a Latin word for a "javelin" or "little dart" which soldiers used to aim at their enemies in battle. So we may call ejaculatory prayer the prayer of little darts! It is a dart which we send up or out toward God Himself. Not to *conquer Him,* but to *break through our own strange unwillingness* to give ourselves to Him. These darts may be single words, or two or three words; words of thanks or of praise or of trust and love; they may be words out of the psalms or familiar hymns. (Only don't let them get mechanical!) They may be sent up to God in school or in the street or anywhere you like. But though they may be very simple, they are worth much; and they will be worth even more if, at some time that suits you, you take the trouble to make a collection of them in a notebook or in your memory. Let there be more prayers of thanks and praise than anything else.

It is a wonderful help to get the habit of thus sending out these little darts. If you have a few ready stored, they will come quickly to your mind in the time of need! You will get the habit of throwing them off at a moment's notice. They will keep reminding you that He is there. For the way to God is always open. His face is always toward us, if we will turn ours to Him.

CHAPTER 25:

## THE LETTER TO THE HEBREWS

It SEEMS a very fitting thing to follow these stories of Old Testament heroes with a few ideas from the writings of a Christian of the first century.

We know from the Book of Acts that soon after our Lord's ascension the central Council of the Church began to look for ways of holding their new converts together. They sent out some of the apostles, and others who seemed well fitted, to visit the new groups already organized in Asia Minor and elsewhere. And because many of those converted in Jerusalem had their homes in remote provinces of the Roman Empire and could rarely be visited, the custom arose of sending circular letters. We know that some of the greatest letter writers were apostles—St. Paul, St. Peter, St. James, St. John. No doubt there were others whose letters have been lost.

Among the letter writers was one who had a wonderful

capacity for making his appeal both personal and effective. No one knows his name: his letter, known as The Epistle to the Hebrews, has been ascribed to St. Paul, to St. Luke, and to St. Barnabas; but none of these names really fits him. The writer of the letter to the Hebrews is unique in his style; and this is natural because he has a very special commission.

He is writing to a number of men and women who had once been Jews, perhaps proselytes. They were thoughtful people and were still living in daily contact with Jews who were dead set against Christianity and were making a stubborn fight to keep the Jewish religion alive. These stubborn defenders of the old faith were holding up to the new Christians the wonderful history of their own people. They were glorifying the pictorial value of the old institutions, their beautiful rites and ceremonies, their power to console those who were still faithful to them.

The Letter to the Hebrews was written at a time when it was still possible for the original Jews to compare the glories of their past with the poverty of the early Christian worship and the small numbers of the primitive Christian Church. The author, writing to the supporters of the early Church, points out that the worship of the Jews had become formal, all on the outside, and that the old sacrifices in the Temple never had power truly to save men from sin. He says the greatest value of the old worship was in what it pointed forward to—as we have so often noted in these stories. Of course he would have admitted that the individual, faithful Jew gained a blessing from his obedience and loyalty to the laws of worship in times when nothing more had been revealed to him; but those days were past.

At the very beginning of his letter, the author sets down, point by point, sharply and clearly, the proper relationship of the Old Testament religion to the New. This is how he begins:

1. *In the old times* God spoke to our forefathers through the words and works of the great prophets.

2. *Now at this time* He has spoken to us in and through His own Son Jesus Christ, who actually *is* the radiant outshining of the glory of God Himself, and the very image of His substance.

3. Jesus Christ came into this world of ours, purified it from sin, and then returned again to the heavenly life from which He came. What angel could do this? Could Abraham? Could Moses? Could David?

Beginning with these claims, the writer of the Epistle goes on to show that Jesus on earth fulfilled all that the Old Testament had shown about the meaning of a prophet, a priest, and a king. He lived and suffered and died as we live and suffer and die; He was tempted in all ways as we are, yet He never sinned. The new Christians were told to notice His work as priest. He stood, and still stands, before God on behalf of man. He represents in the heavenly life all mankind, united to God through His work of redemption.

His life, His passion, His resurrection were all on the scene of human history. On the Cross He offered Himself for us, once for all. But not as a great deed which happened *outside* us, something we gazed upon. It did not leave us as we were.

On the night on which He was betrayed He said, "This is *the new covenant* in my blood!" Look back to the hour of the old covenant with Moses on Sinai, when the people were sprinkled with the blood of the sacrificed animals. Jesus Christ has offered us the blood of His sacrifice. He has made us partakers of it and, with it, partakers of His life. In the hour of sacramental communion we receive the Divine Life and give our own lives back again to Him.

This is a summary of what the author of the Letter to the Hebrews teaches us of the meaning of the sacrifice of Christ. It is drawn out with great care as he describes how our Lord in His life and passion fulfills all that was once symbolized in the great Jewish Day of Atonement.

Then the author turns again to his hearers. "It is hard for you to believe all this," he says in effect. "It seems to you to be a day of small things. What you need is *faith* in the full, Old Testament sense of *trust*. Trust in God who keeps His Promises, because He is the great Amen, who abides forever."

Then he asks them to go back with him to their own history, and reminds them of their saints and heroes who, under much harder circumstances, trusted God and came out victoriously from all their trials. This is the famous eleventh chapter of Hebrews.

He builds up his point with stories from the very beginning of history. He takes them all the way back to the Creation and even further—back to the unfathomable depths of the Being of God where our human minds cannot follow. Here faith finds its rest only in the Divine Revelation. "He spake the word and it was done." This kind of faith is not something we can argue ourselves into; it is really a gift of God Himself; but it has its foundation in the moment when man owns himself to be the child of God and looks up to see what God may have to say to him.

We are reminded of how man was set in a new world with new duties. He has his proper sphere in work, family life, social life. If life is God's gift, he must give God lordship over it. If he does this in simple gratitude, not as to a tyrant, he will find a wide and wonderful way opening out between himself and God, and between himself and his fellowmen.

So, first on the list of heroic stories, we are given the allegory of Cain and Abel. Each brother has his own earthen altar, and each puts his gift upon it. Human sacrifice is not allowed to Hebrews, but it is expected that a sacrifice to God will be a gift of value. Abel brings a lamb from the flock; Cain, the produce of his fields. One gift, we are told, was "accepted"; the other not. Abel had brought what through all later ages was regarded as the gift God had always asked from man. Abel, says our author, "by faith" brought the offering that in his time was thought most pleasing to God. Had God told him so and not told Cain? That seems unthinkable in the light of what even in earliest times was considered worthy of God. There must, therefore, have been some failure of obedience on Cain's part, and it developed into the sin of murder. But the whole story brings to the forefront the outstanding revelation that man's life is *not his own;* that it belongs to God and is not at his own disposal. And this makes clearer the meaning of the second story the letter writer reviews. Enoch was taken away from this life without dying because, while all the men around him were living for themselves and following their own ways, he "walked with God" and *"was well-pleasing to him."*

And here is inserted the great classical definition of faith: "Now faith is the assurance of things hoped for, the conviction of things not seen." "Without faith it is impossible to please him. For whoever would draw near to God must believe that he exists and that he rewards those who seek him." Another way of saying this is that God keeps His promises of help to those who believe He will. Through faith, the things we "hope for" are realized (take on substance). (Hebrews 11:1 and 6)

Having heard that definition, we need not go through the whole list of names the letter writer mentions. Many will be found in this book, for the letter refers to all of them—kings, priests, and prophets—who pleased God because they believed He would not fail them. The man of faith depends upon the faithfulness of God.

Through this grand catalogue we see the connection between faith, obedience, love, and surrender of the will. God calls all men to give themselves to Him because their life comes from Him and goes back to Him again. He calls a few of the great ones to give themselves entirely, all they have and are. And to them He gives sometimes a vision of the far future: "Therefore God is not ashamed to be called their God, for he has prepared for them a city."

The thirteenth chapter of the letter is a wonderful summary of the Christian life. In its main features the Christian life has the same obligations that life had under the Jewish law, but it is glorified by being centered all the way on the love of Jesus Christ. On the ethical side, there is the duty of hospitality, with a special care for complete strangers; sympathy with the afflicted; faithfulness to marriage vows; the avoidance of too much love for money; respect to all in lawful authority, especially the rulers of the Church. All these things are *well-pleasing* to God, and all rest upon the central act of faith which this writer puts before us in what is perhaps the best-known verse of his letter: "Jesus Christ is the same yesterday and today and for ever." Jesus Christ: His holy Name links up all the hopes and promises of the past and future: the Name of Love—God with us— Immanuel.

And we are reminded also that the duty of the love of God includes corporate worship. "And let us consider how to stir up one another to love and good works, not neglecting to meet together." (Hebrews 10:24–25) For "we have an altar" at which the old Jews have no right to eat: we must pay it honor. (Hebrews 13:10)

Time will bring changes of form to our worship, but some parts of it will never change. The sacrifice of praise and thanksgiving, through Jesus Christ our Lord, in the Eucharist, is one; the duty of brotherly kindness is another: "for with such sacrifices God is *well pleased*." (Hebrews 13:16)

The letter ends with a lovely blessing in the best Christian manner:

"Now may the God of peace who brought again from the dead our Lord Jesus, the great shepherd of the sheep, by the blood of the eternal covenant, equip you with everything good that you may do his will, working in you that which is pleasing in his sight, through Jesus Christ, to whom be glory for ever and ever. Amen."

# index

# INDEX

Aaron, 52, 60
Abner, 95
Abraham, 25–32, 37, 40, 43, 47,
   130, 159, 165
  God of, 51, 115
Absalom, 100–101
Acts, Book of, 153, 163
Adam and Eve, 10, 11, 12, 13,
   159
Agreement, 31, 32
Ahab, 111, 114, 116, 120–121
Ahaz, 139–141
Alexander the Great, 72, 152
Altar, 29, 42, 57, 115, 136, 151,
   153, 169
Amen, 166
Amos, 127–130
Angel, 29, 40, 72, 77, 165
Anoint, 33, 86, 91, 96, 119
Apostles, 163
Ark, Noah's. See Noah
Ark of the Covenant, 61, 62,
   68, 70, 81, 83–85, 96, 100
Assyria, 15, 21, 134, 141
Atonement, Day of, 166

Baal, 112–116
Babylon, 17, 33, 146

Babylonia, 15, 20, 21
Baptism, 154, 156
Bathsheba, 99
Benedictus, 30, 155
Bethel, 40, 42, 81
Bethlehem, 21, 94
Bible
  importance of, 9, 12, 158
  reading the, 4, 159
  theme of, 5, 21
Birthright, 38
Blessing, 26, 28, 38–39, 164,
   169
Brothers, 45, 47
Brother's keeper, 14
Burning bush, 50

Cain and Abel, 13–14, 167
Calf, golden, 60
Call, 25, 138
Calvary, 154
Canaan, 26, 47, 53, 64, 70, 112
Captivity, 17, 33, 135, 146
Challenge, 114, 161
Champion, 78
Chariot of fire, 123, 124
Cheat. See Deceit
Cherubs, 84, 137

Chosen people, 20, 31, 129, 155
Christ, the, 34, 35. *See also*
  Jesus Christ
Christian, 145, 152, 153, 154,
  155, 156, 164, 168
Christian charity, 132
Christmas, 21
Church, 21, 155, 164
Coat, Joseph's, 44, 45
Communion, 166
Confession, 71
Conscience, 40, 79, 91
Contest, 116
Covenant, 18, 32, 47, 56, 60,
  136, 154
Covet, 38, 59
Creation, 10, 11, 13, 166
Creator, 10
Cross, 165
Cyrus, King of Persia, 21, 33,
  148–149, 150

Daniel, 148
David, 32, 34, 85, 88–104, 165
Dead Sea, 64, 69
Death
  of Absalom, 101
  of Elijah, 123
  of Moses, 63
  of Saul, 92
Deceit, 40, 41
Delilah, 78
Deliverer, 32, 33, 34
Disciples, 34, 154, 160
Dream
  Jacob's, 40

Dream—*(Continued)*
  Joseph's, 44
  Pharaoh's, 46
Duty to parents, 57, 91

Earthquakes, 69, 70, 118
Easter, 145
Egypt, 15, 20, 21, 45, 46, 49,
  50, 52, 54, 76, 129, 141
Election, 86
Eli, 81, 82, 83, 84
Elijah, 113–123
Elisha, 119, 121–125
Elkanah, 81
Esau, 37–40, 42
Eucharist, 166, 169
Euphrates River, 15
Excavations, 9, 16, 18, 25, 71,
  76
Excuses, 118
Exile, 146, 150
Exodus, 53
Ezra, 150, 152

Faith, 25, 30, 37, 56, 61, 99,
  117, 130, 146, 157, 161,
  166, 167, 168
False witness, 46, 121
Famine, 46
Family, 38, 91
Father, 38, 91
Fickleness, 116, 132
Fiery furnace, 148
First-born, 53
First fruits, 57, 70
Flood, 16–19

Forgiveness, 41, 48, 62, 138
Freedom, 3, 4
Free will, 11
Friendship, 90–91, 98

Galilee, 34, 141
Garden of Eden, 13, 158
Generosity, 91, 98
Genesis, 10, 11, 25
Gentile, 35, 153, 156
Gideon, 80
God
  answer of, 42, 115, 126
  demands of, 17, 26, 72, 99,
    126
  friends of, 30, 158
  gift of, 33, 59, 78, 166, 167
  image of, 10, 158
  judgment of, 100, 130
  love of, 127, 130, 131–134,
    146, 158
  mercy of, 28, 32, 99, 130,
    146
  messages of, 82, 83, 106, 113,
    134, 138, 139
  obedience to, 33, 141
  plan of, 88, 146
  presence of, 32, 51, 60, 83,
    118, 123, 138, 158
  promise of, 18, 26, 40, 42–
    43, 47, 83, 140, 141, 166
  purpose of, 4, 11, 21, 37, 144,
    145
  voice of, 40, 51, 52, 67, 82,
    117–119, 138, 139
  way of, 18, 28, 139

Goliath, 89–90
Gomorrah, 28
Good Samaritan, 14
Gospel, 21, 153
Grace, 132
Greek, 152
Greeks, 72, 74
Grief, 99, 101

Hannah, 81–82
Heathen, 10, 18, 99. *See also*
  Baal
Hebrews, 21, 25, 26, 33, 43, 49,
  50, 51, 55, 57, 61, 69, 98,
  146, 167
Hero, 77, 98
History, 11, 20, 21, 25, 40, 134,
  144, 145, 164, 165
Holy Ark. *See* Ark of the
  Covenant
Holy Communion. *See*
  Eucharist
Holy Land, 61
*Holy Scriptures*, 10
Holy Spirit, 9, 155
Hosea, 127, 130–134
House of David, 34, 103, 141,
  155
Hymns, 30, 155, 161
Hypocrisy, 130

Idols, 60, 72, 84, 106, 146
Image of God, 10, 158
Incarnation, 5
Ingratitude, 131, 132
Isaac, 28–29, 37–43

Isaiah, 21, 134, 135–143
Israel, 36, 43, 49, 51, 108, 129,
    131, 135, 139, 145, 154
Israelites, 17, 56, 59, 68, 83, 87,
    88. *See also* Hebrews

Jacob, 37–47
Jealousy, 14, 90, 95, 96
Jehovah, 51, 57, 77, 99, 103,
    122, 128, 141
Jericho, 65, 66, 70
Jerusalem, 96, 100, 101, 104,
    142, 149, 151, 153
Jesus Christ, 21, 34, 35, 72, 141,
    145, 154, 160, 165, 166,
    168, 169
Jews, 35, 36, 77, 148, 153, 154,
    164, 169
Jezebel, 111, 116, 120–121
Joab, 95–96, 100–102
John the Baptist, 30, 34
Jonathan, 90–91, 93, 98
Jordan, 28, 59, 64, 100, 113,
    122, 125
Joseph, 40
Joshua, 32, 60, 63, 65–73, 151
Judah, 108, 128–129, 135, 139
Judge, 85
Justice, 130

King, 85, 86, 87, 94, 98, 111,
    154, 165
Kingdom, 95, 102, 108
Kingdom of God, 144

Laban, 40–42
Languages, 14, 152

Last Supper, 154
Law, 57, 104, 127, 146, 164, 168
Leah, 41, 44
Legend, 9, 11, 25, 76, 77
Leprosy, 124–125
Lions, 148
Lord. *See* God *and* Jehovah
Lost tribes, 134
Lot, 26–28
Love, 62, 98, 130–134, 168
Loyalty, 95, 148, 161, 164
Luxury, 105

Magnificat, 30, 82
Mesopotamia, 15, 141
Messiah, 33–35, 154
Messianic promise, 33–36
Miracles, 65, 67–70
Mission, 126
Missionary, 21
Monuments, 76, 84
Moses, 32, 50–66, 104, 116,
    122, 160, 165, 166
Mount Carmel, 114, 116, 117
Mount Sinai (Horeb), 50, 53,
    56, 57, 60, 117, 166
Murder, 59, 167
Music, 88
Mustard seed, 157
Myth, 10, 11

Name, 51, 72, 89, 151, 169
Nation, 56, 59, 104
*National Geographic*, 18, 71
Nazareth, 34
Nazirite, 77–78
Near East, 76, 152

Nehemiah, 151–152
Neighbor, 14
New Covenant, 154, 165
New Testament, 5, 21, 132, 141, 165
Noah, 17, 18, 159
Northern kingdom. *See* Israel
Nunc dimittus, 156

Obedience, 30, 32, 164, 167, 168
Obligation, 32
Offering, 13, 14, 29, 70, 130, 167
Old Testament, 5, 11, 21, 127, 141, 152, 155, 165

Palestine, 26, 64
Parable, 11, 14, 132
Passover, 53, 141
Penitence, 71, 99, 121
Persia, 15. *See also* Cyrus
Pharaoh, 51, 52, 54
Pharaoh's daughter, 50
Pharisee, 35
Philistines, 74, 76–80, 83, 85, 87, 88, 92, 142
Poor, the, 127, 129, 135
Potiphar, 45–46
Prayer, 10, 62, 81–82, 83, 99, 158–162
Priest, 34, 68, 84, 136, 153, 165
Promise, 34, 73, 154. *See also* God
Promised Land, 31, 33, 36, 61, 62, 66, 70

Prophet, 21, 32, 35, 63, 82–83, 97, 99, 111, 113, 126, 127, 130, 131, 139, 146, 165
Proselytes, 153, 164
Psalms, 11, 69, 103, 145, 154, 158, 159, 161
Punishment, 60, 61, 115, 128, 129

Rachel, 41, 44
Rain, 112–116
Rainbow, 17, 18, 156
Ravens, 113
Rebecca, 38–40
Red Sea, 53, 56, 67
Redemption, 20, 21, 34, 35, 154, 165
Relationship, 5, 131
Religion, 102, 112, 141, 146, 152, 153
    and conduct, 135
Repentance, 154
Resurrection, 154, 165
Retreat, 60
Revelation, 9, 166, 167
Right, 161
Righteous, 17, 28, 99, 130
Roman Empire, 34, 153, 163
Ruler, 10
Ruth, 80

Sabbath, 57
Sacrifice, 14, 29, 53, 57, 95, 112, 114, 136, 141, 152, 164, 166, 167, 169

Saint
John the Baptist, 30, 113, 155
John, 154
Luke, 154, 164
Paul, 35, 72, 155, 159, 160, 163, 164
Salvation, 65, 151, 155, 156
Samaritans, 14, 151
Samson, 77–80
Samuel, 82–87
Saul, 86–93
Scriptures, 10
writing of, 10, 77, 106, 146, 152
Separation from God, 11
Shiloh, 81, 84, 85
Simeon, 156
Sin, 11, 18, 28, 98, 99, 129, 131, 145, 158, 164
Slavery, 45, 49, 127
Social life, 13, 59, 167
Sodom, 28
Solomon, 102, 104–107
Southern kingdom. *See* Judah
Spies, 61
Spirit, 158
Spoiled child, 44, 100
Suffering, 18, 139
Symbol, 18, 33, 57, 90
Syria, 123, 124, 128, 139, 153, 166

Tabernacle, 61, 62, 81, 82
Tablets of stone, 60, 61, 84
Taxation, 106, 127

Temple, 96, 103, 104, 136, 151, 153
Temptation, 29, 62, 112, 116
Ten Commandments, 57, 84, 113, 127
Thanksgiving, 82, 96
Tigris River, 15
Tombs, 16
Training for God's purpose, 20, 40, 42, 48, 65, 123
Trojans, 74
Troy, 74
Trust, 66, 140, 161, 166
Twelve tribes of Israel, 35, 43, 52, 57, 115

Ur, 16, 18, 19, 25

Vengeance, 95
Vineyard, Naboth's, 120
Virgin Mary, 30, 34, 82
Vision, 26, 42, 123, 136, 141

Walking with God, 26, 159–161, 168
War of nerves, 70
Wilderness, 54, 60, 61, 65, 68, 129
Wisdom, 105–106
Witch of Endor, 92
Word of God, 10
Worship, 81, 96, 99, 104, 112, 127, 146, 169
services of, 61, 62, 136

Zechariah, 30, 136, 155